Piano/Conductor Score

a new MUSICAL

Music by JOHN CLIFTON

Lyrics by JOHN CLIFTON and BEN TARVER

Book by BEN TARVER

Adapted from a play by
ASHLEY DUKES

Copyright © 1966, 2011 John Clifton, Donald Goldman and Ben Tarver
ALL RIGHTS RESERVED INCLUDING PUBLIC PERFORMANCE FOR PROFIT

Stock and Amateur Rights Licensed by SAMUEL FRENCH, NEW YORK

REVISED EDITION

Precipice Music
A subsidiary of Foley Square Books

MischiefTheMusical.com

Man with A Load of Mischief Copyright 1966, 2011 by John Clifton, Donald H. Goldman and Ben Tarver.

All Rights Reserved. International copyright Secured

No part of this book, including music, lyrics, text and graphics, may be reproduced in any form or by any means, electronic or mechanical, including photocopying, recording, or by an information storage and retrieval system, without written permission in writing from the Publisher. Unauthorized copying, arranging, adapting, recording or public performance is an infringement of copyright. Infringers are liable under the law.

Publication date, Revised Edition: April 2011   ISBN 978-0-9760846-5-5

Additional copies and information:

Visit the show's Web site at *MischiefTheMusical.com* for further information and to order additional copies of this score.

Foley Square Books
P. O. Box 20548
Park West Station
New York, NY 10025

Man with a Load of Mischief

Music by John Clifton
Lyrics by John Clifton and Ben Tarver
Book by Ben Tarver

Based upon the play
The Man With A Load of Mischief by Ashley Dukes

Produced by Donald H. Goldman
First performance November 1966, Jan Hus Playhouse, New York

Directed by Tom Gruenewald
Musical Direction by Sande Campbell
Choreography by Noel Schwartz
Scenery and Lighting by Joan Larkey
Costumes by Volavkova
Production Stage Manager–Gail Bell

Cast of Characters
(in order of appearance)

THE INNKEEPER	Tom Noel
THE WIFE	Lesslie Nicol
THE MAID	Alice Cannon
THE MAN	Reid Shelton
THE LORD	Raymond Thorne
THE LADY	Virginia Vestoff

PIANO/HARPSICHORD/CELESTE	Sande Campbell
CLARINET/FLUTE	Larry Abel
'CELLO	David Levine

TABLE OF CONTENTS

ACT ONE

1.	Overture	1
2.	Wayside Inn	7
3.	The Rescue	10
4.	Entrance Polonaise	18
4A.	Wayside Inn Exit	20
4B.	Friend #1	21
4C.	Scene Change - After Friend #1	22
4D.	Underscore before "Goodbye My Sweet"	23
5.	Good-bye, My Sweet!	24
5A.	Scene Change and Underscore after "Good-bye"	34
6.	Romance!	35
6B.	After "Romance"	53
7.	Lover Lost	54
7A.	After "Lover" Scene Change	59
8.	Once You've Had A Little Taste	60
8A.	Friend #2	72
9.	Hulla-Baloo-Balay	73
10.	"Once You've Had A Little Taste" – REPRISE	82
11.	Dinner Minuet	84
11A.	After "Minuet"	87
12.	You'd Be Amazed	88
13.	With A Friend Like You	101
14.	The Hour Is Late	106
15.	Come To The Masquerade	108
15A.	After "Masquerade"	114
15B.	Masquerade Waltz #1	115
15C.	Masquerade Waltz #2	118
16.	Man With A Load Of Mischief	119
16A.	"Masquerade Reprise" Intro	124
17.	"Masquerade" REPRISE	125

ACT TWO

18.	Entr'acte/Curtain Music	128
19.	What Style!	129
19A.	"What Style! Fragment	142
20.	A Wonder	143
21.	Make Way For My Lady	148
21A.	"Make Way" Playoff	153
22.	Forget!	154
22A.	"Forget" REPRISE	158
23.	Any Other Way	159
24.	Before "Rag Doll"	165
24A.	Little Rag Doll	167
24B.	After "Rag Doll"	170
25.	"Romance" REPRISE	171
25B.	"Man With A Load Of Mischief" REPRISE	178
26.	Sextet	180
27.	"Make Way" REPRISE	185
27A.	Coach Underscore	190
27B	Final Curtain	194
27C	Bow Music	195
28	Exit Music	197

Overture

Man With A Load Of Mischief

Andante Maestoso

Copyright © 1966-2008 John Clifton and Ben Tarver

Wayside Inn

[The Innkeeper]

The Rescue

[Wife, Innkeeper]

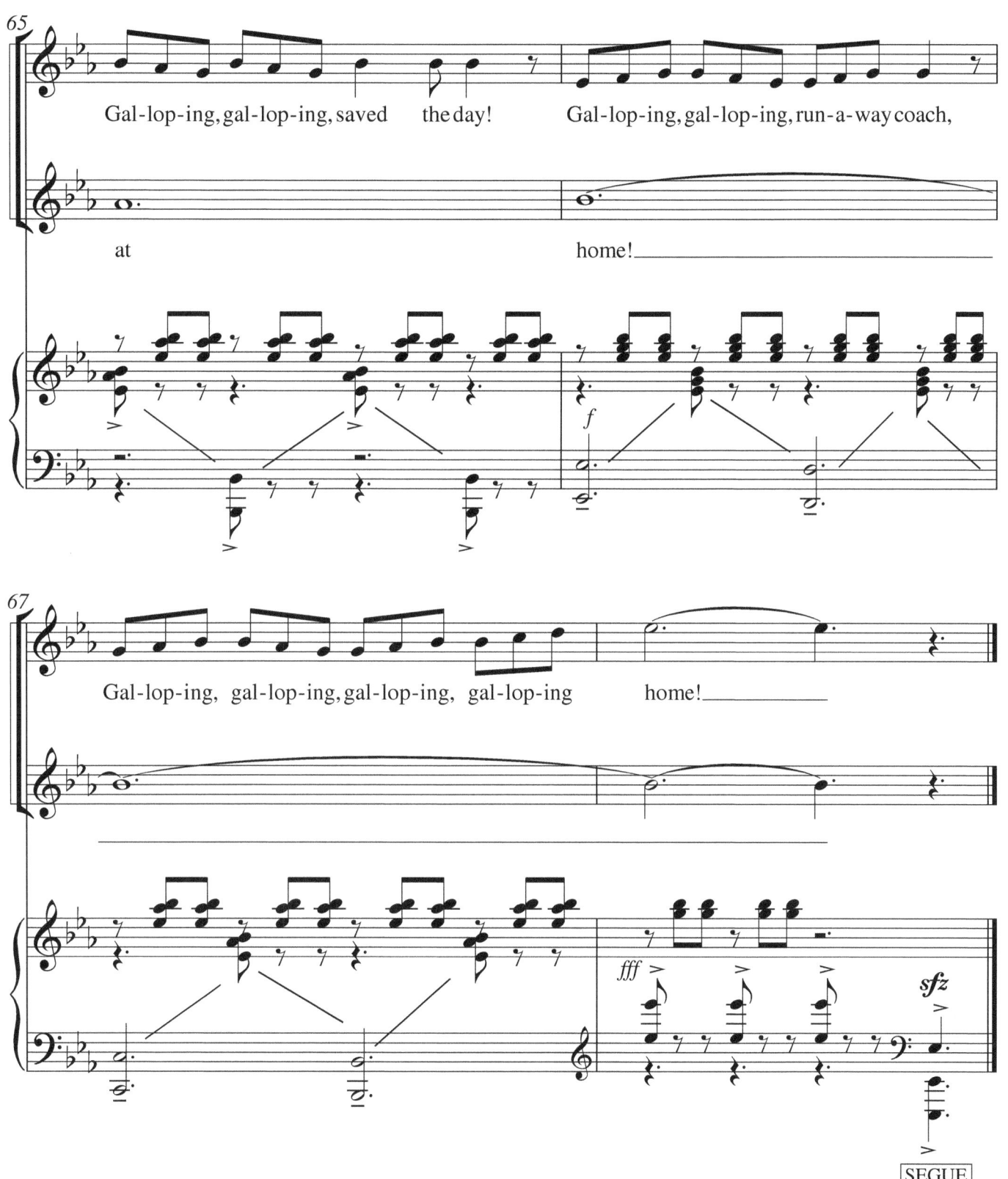

Entrance Polonaise

Wayside Inn Exit

4-A

[Innkeeper]

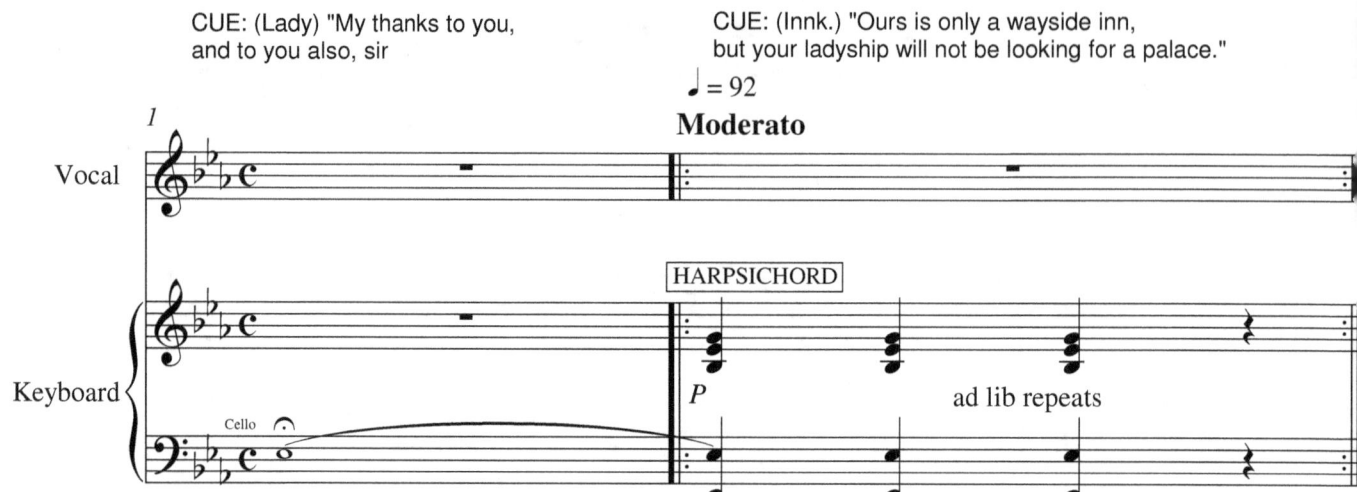

Scene Change After Friend #1

4-C

Underscore Before "Good-bye My Sweet"

4-D

CUE: (Lady) "One travels faster alone."

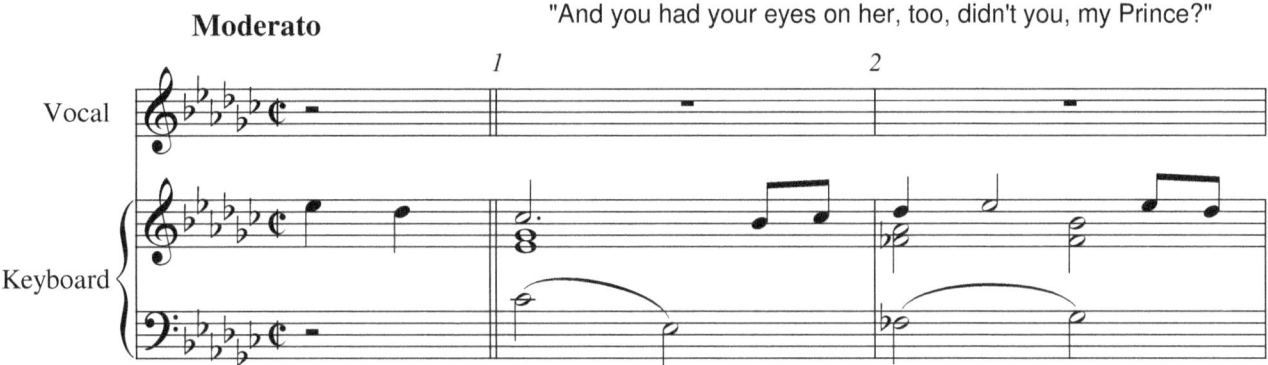

SEGUE AS ONE

Scene Change and Underscore
After Good-bye My Sweet

5-A

START AFTER BLACKOUT

Moderato

Harpsichord

(Stop when traveler is open)

34

Romance

[Innkeeper, Wife, Lord, Maid]

44
all, Now, if you are poor that's a com-mon ad - vance But if you are
tenuto
50
rich it's ro mance! Romance! Ro - mance! Ro - mance! A
55
dash - ing and smash - ing ro - mance

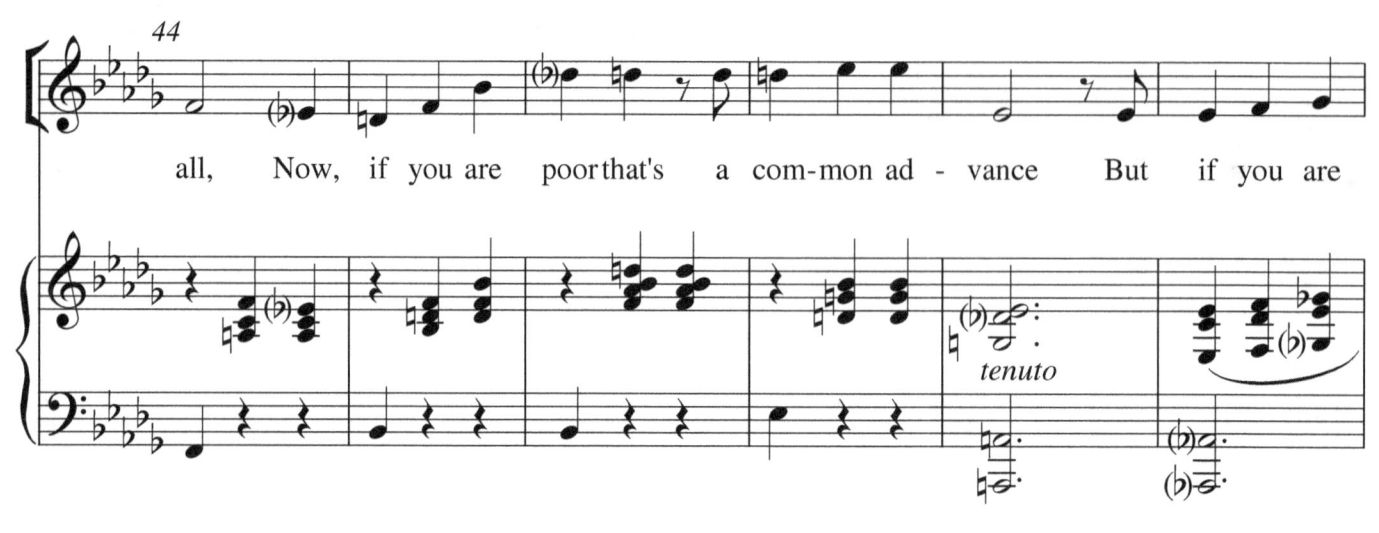

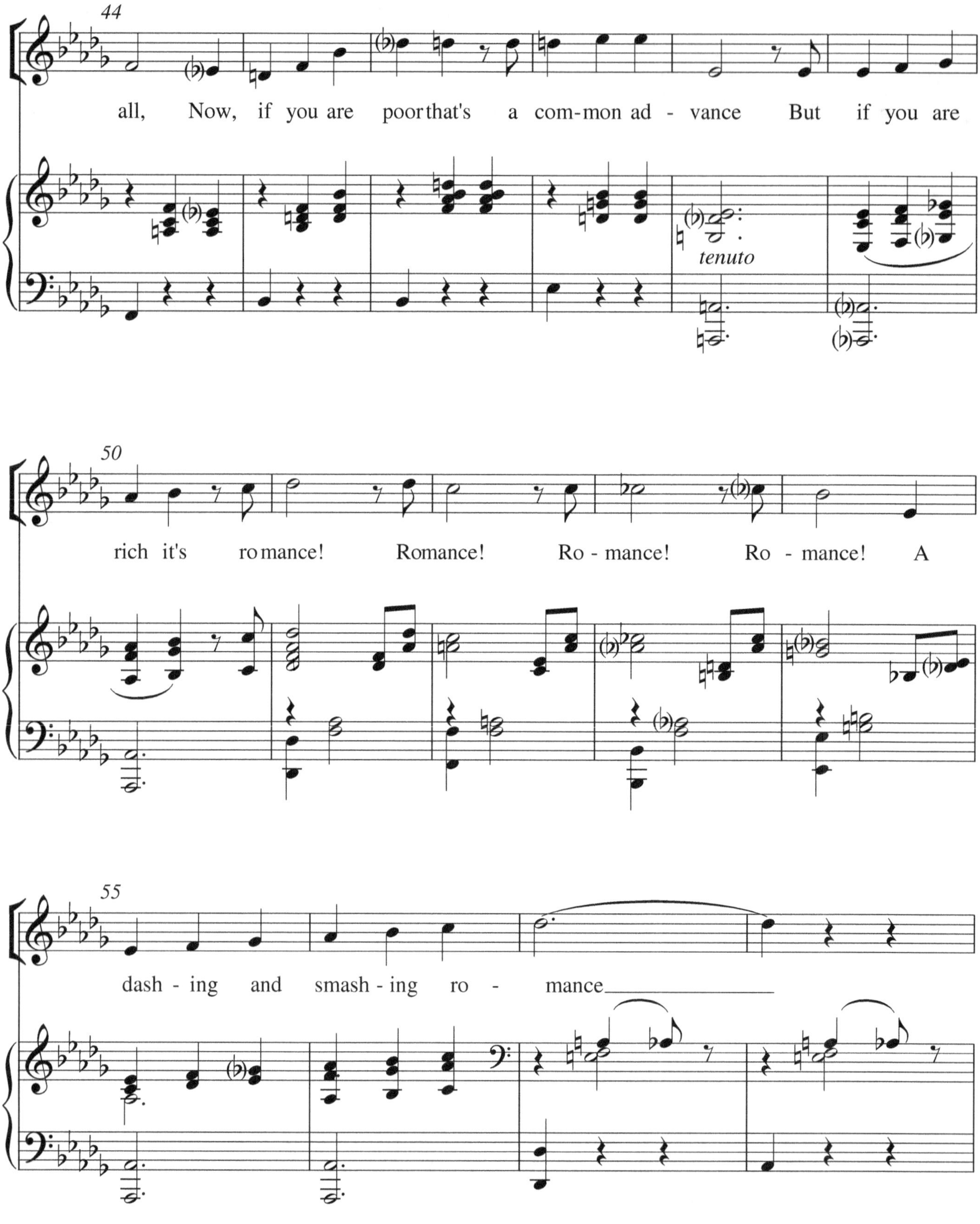

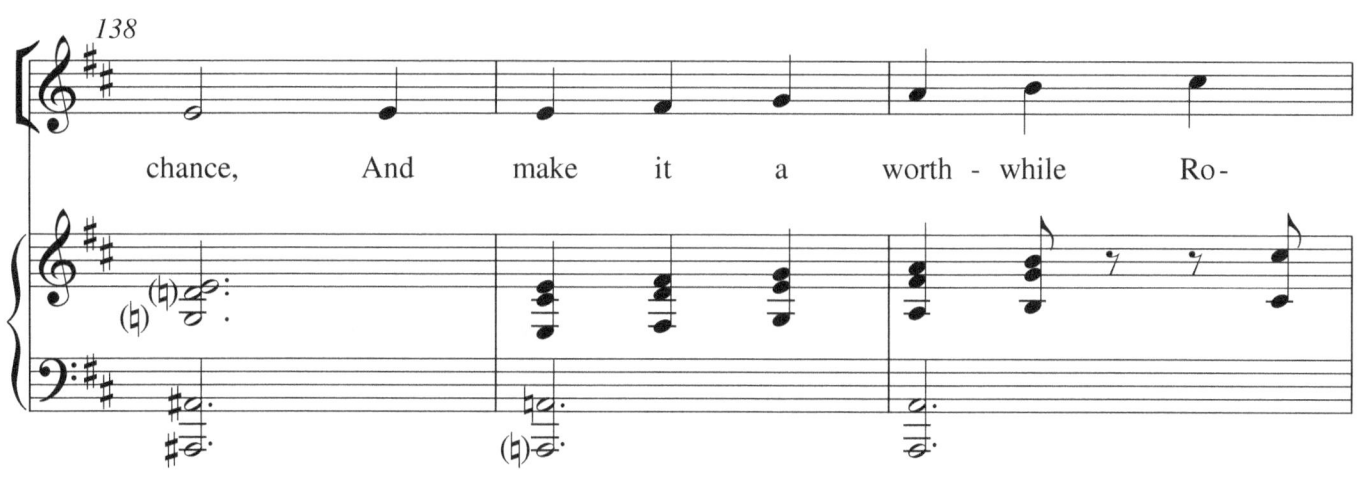

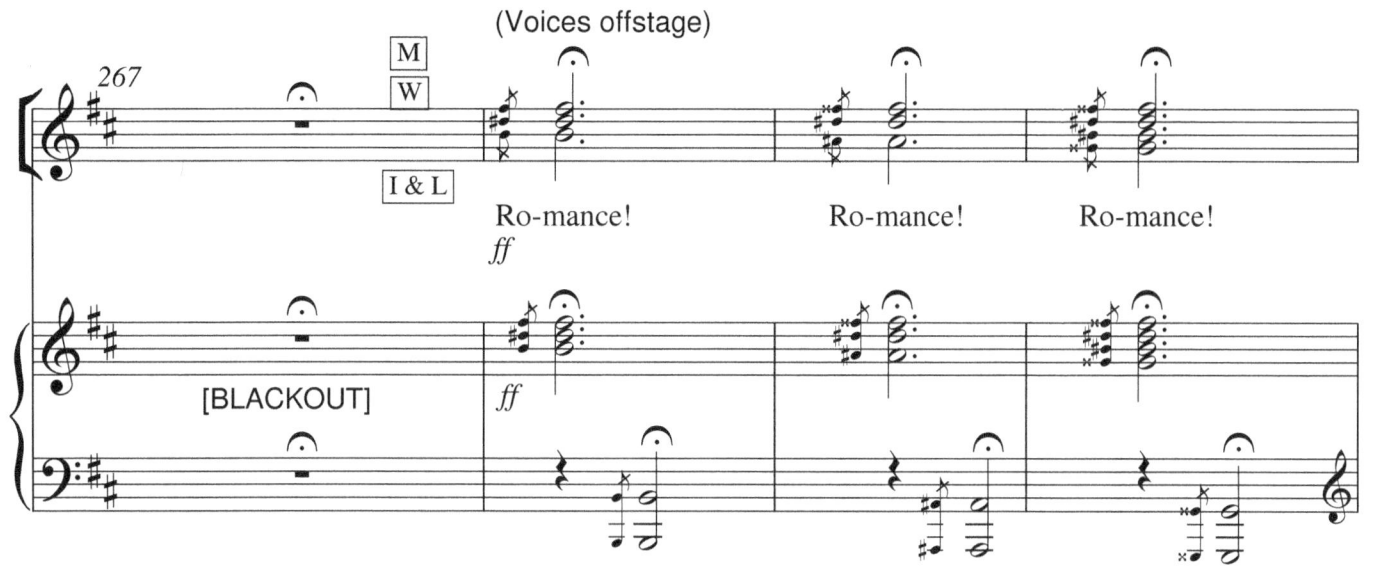
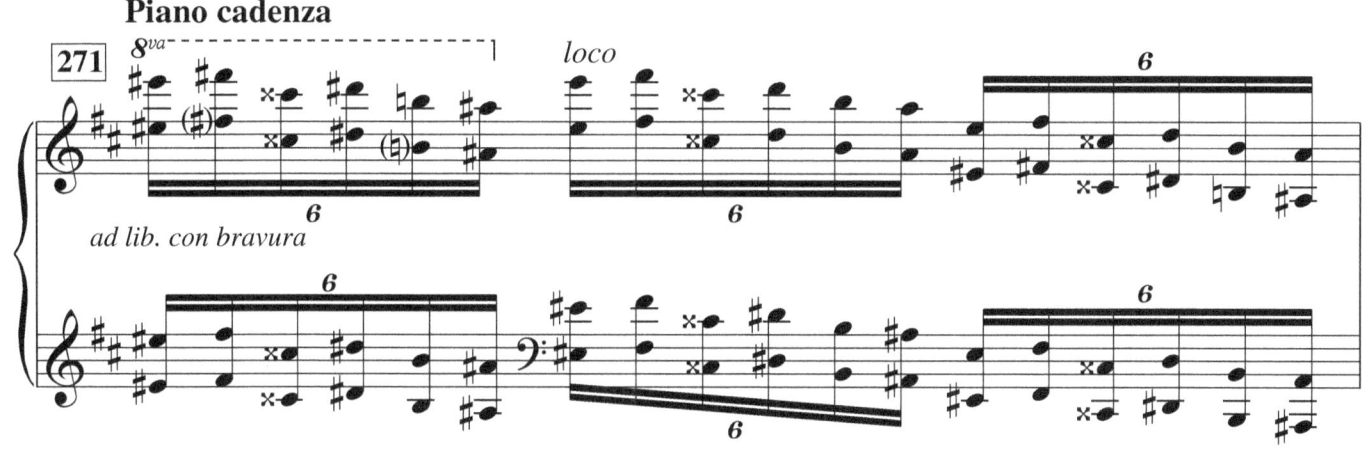

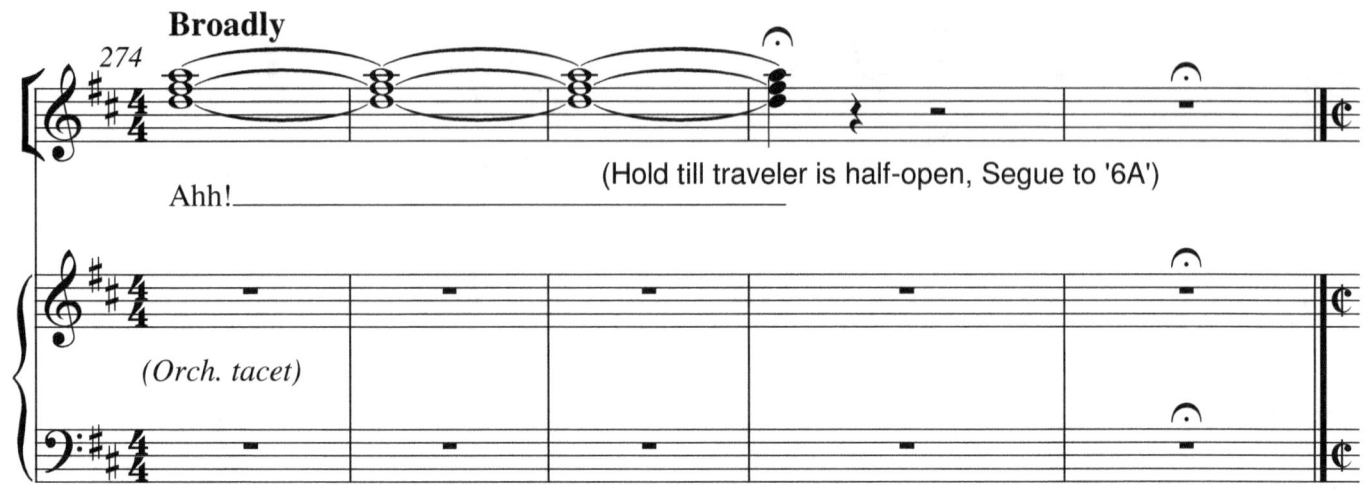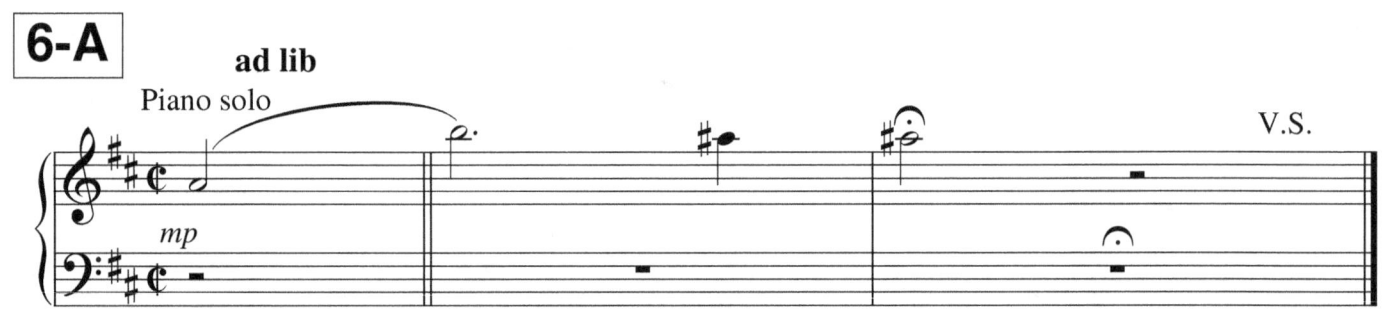

6B

After Romance

Cue: (Lights)

♩ = 132

Allegro

flute

Keyboard (tacet)

cello

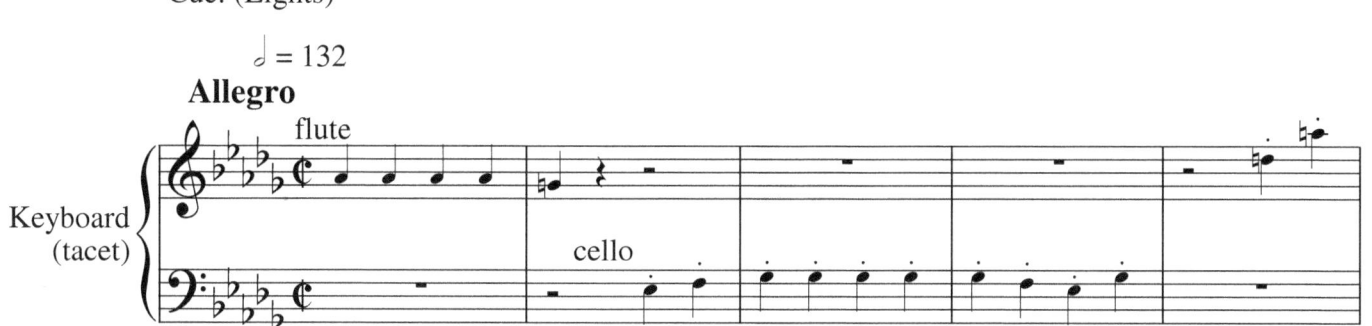

Repeats. Off on "Hold there!"

CUT when lady is startled.

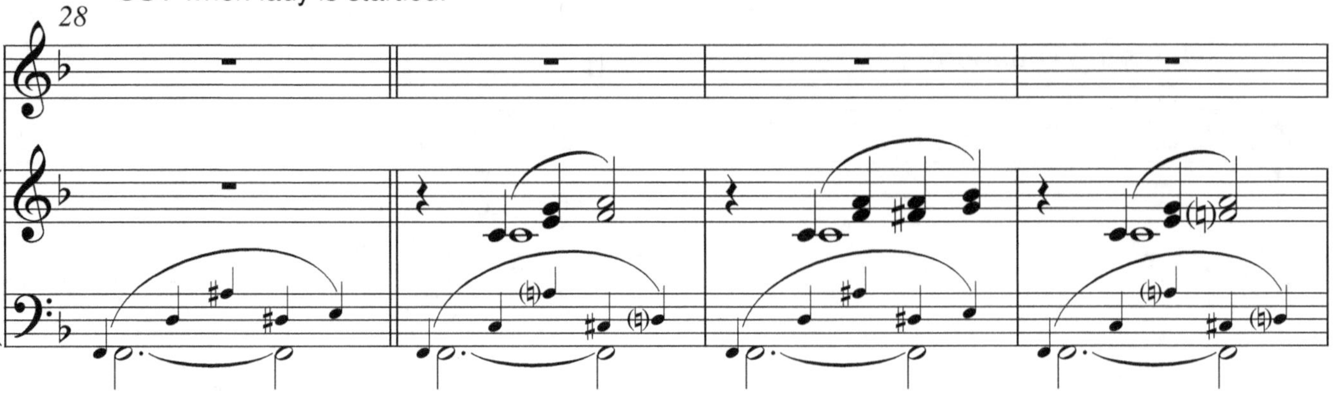
28

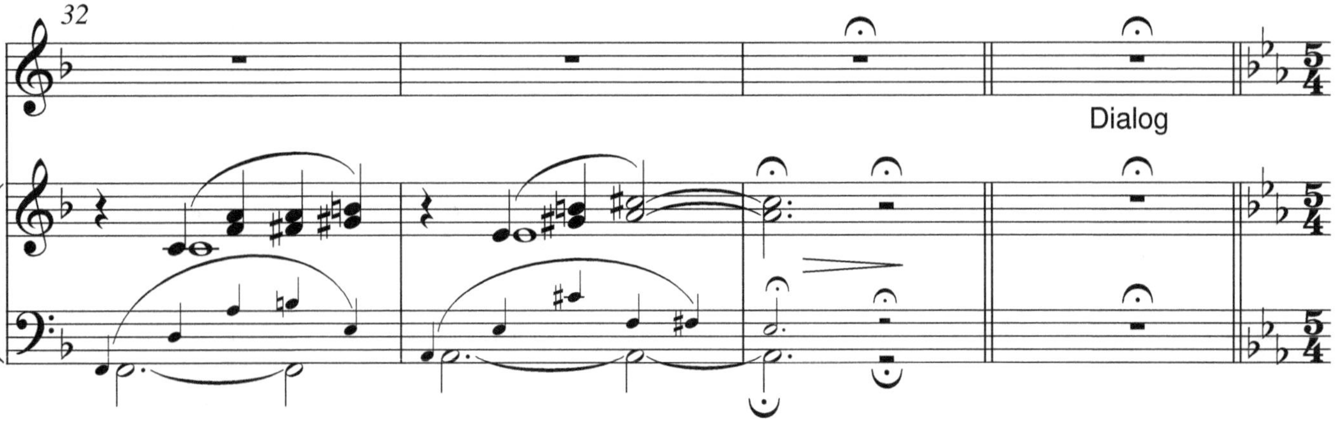
32
Dialog

Cue (Lady):
"You are too kind, my Lord."

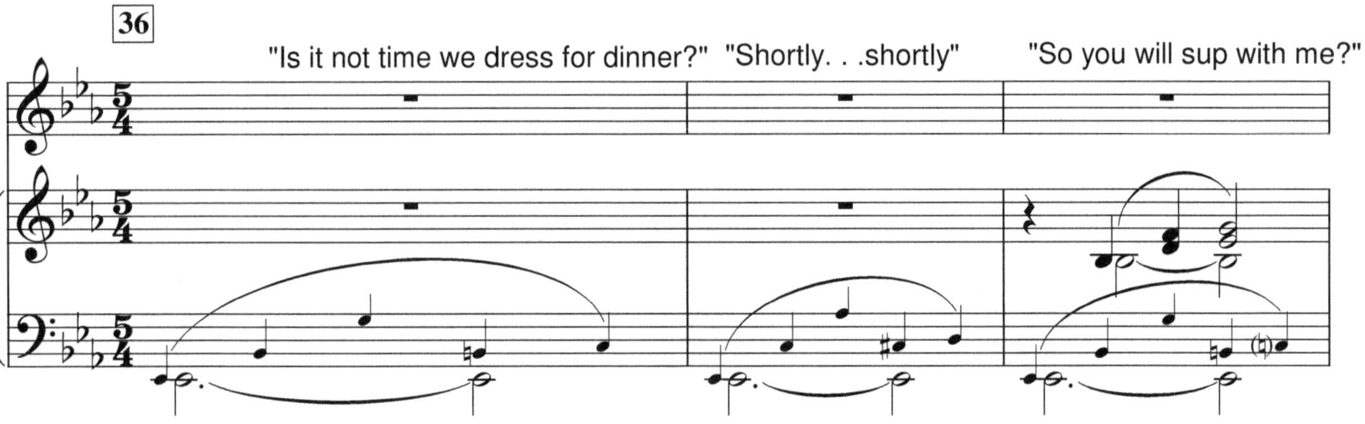
36
"Is it not time we dress for dinner?"
"Shortly. . .shortly"
"So you will sup with me?"

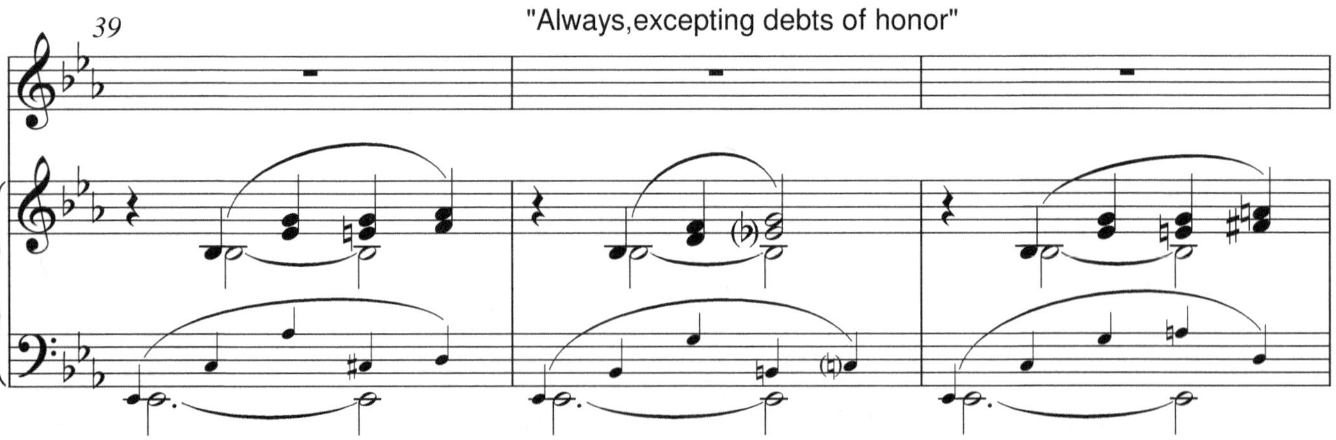
39
"Always,excepting debts of honor"

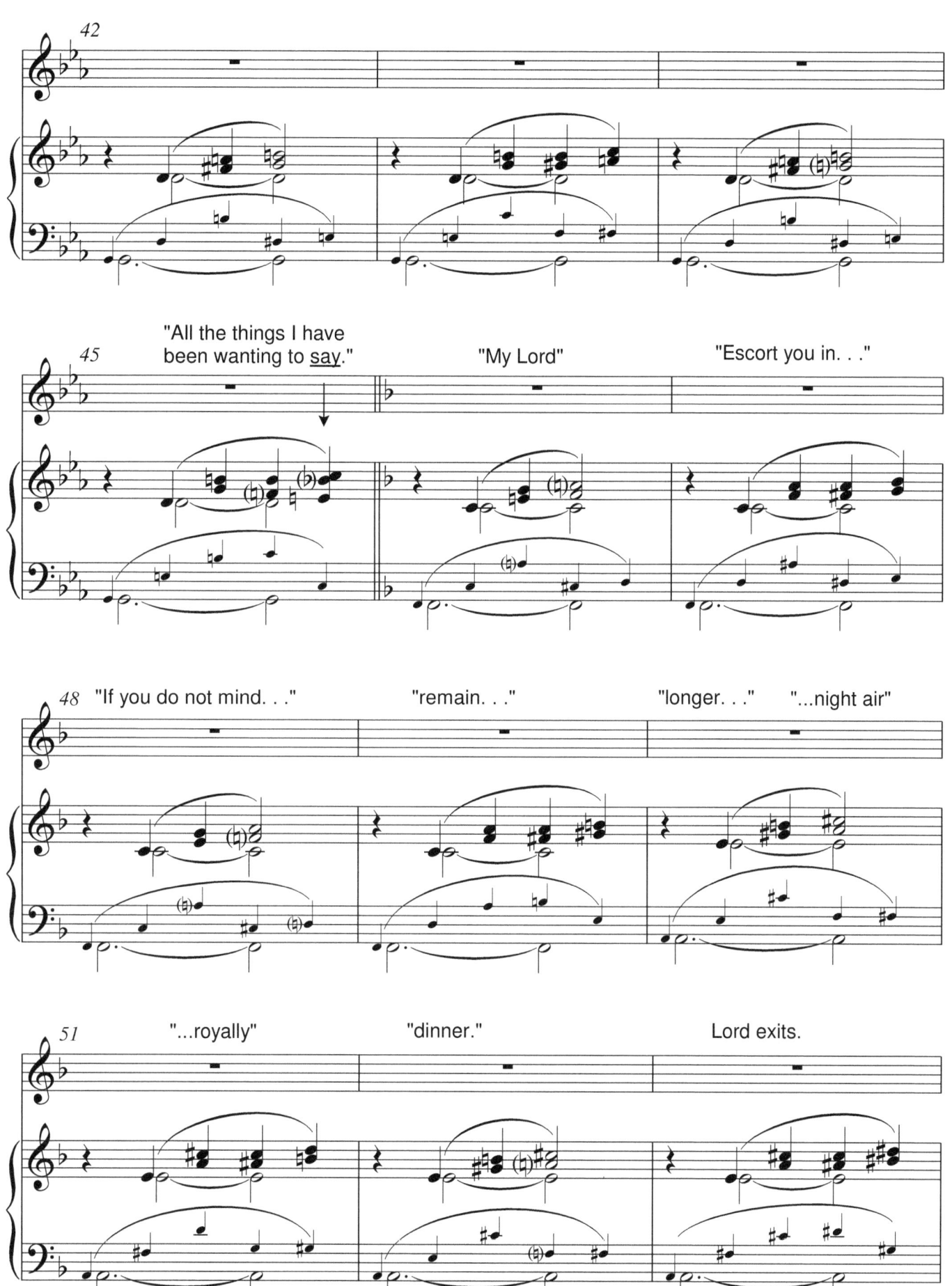

7-A

After Lover – Scene Change

Once You've Had A Little Taste

WARN (Maid): "...cramped in a coach."
CUE (Maid): "...fine life at Bath."

[Maid]

Mu-sic in the gar-dens ev'-ry night_____ Par-ties in the pal-ace

left and right_____ Fan-cy din-ners when you sit to

60

Hulla-Baloo-Balay

[The Man]

CUE (Maid): "...a real nobleman now..."

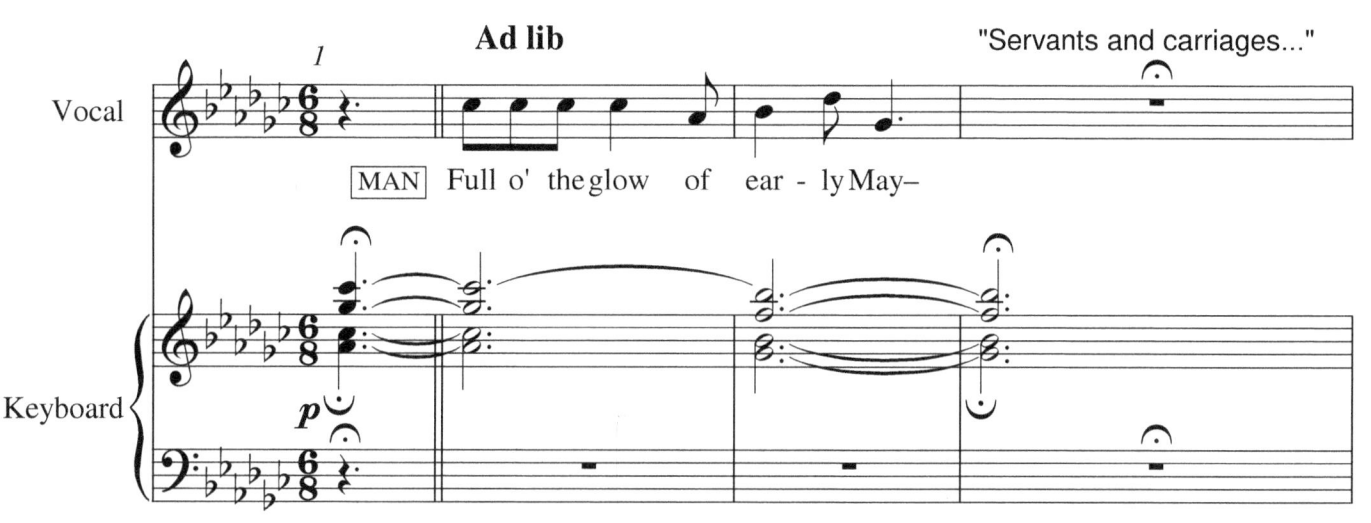

Little Taste (Reprise)

[Wife, Innkeeper, Maid]

CUE (Wife): "I remember what it was like."

Dinner Minuet

CUE: Direct segue from previous

After Minuet
[Underscore]

11-A

You'd Be Amazed
[Lord, Lady, Man]

CUE (LORD): "To leave the world gracefully requires breeding."

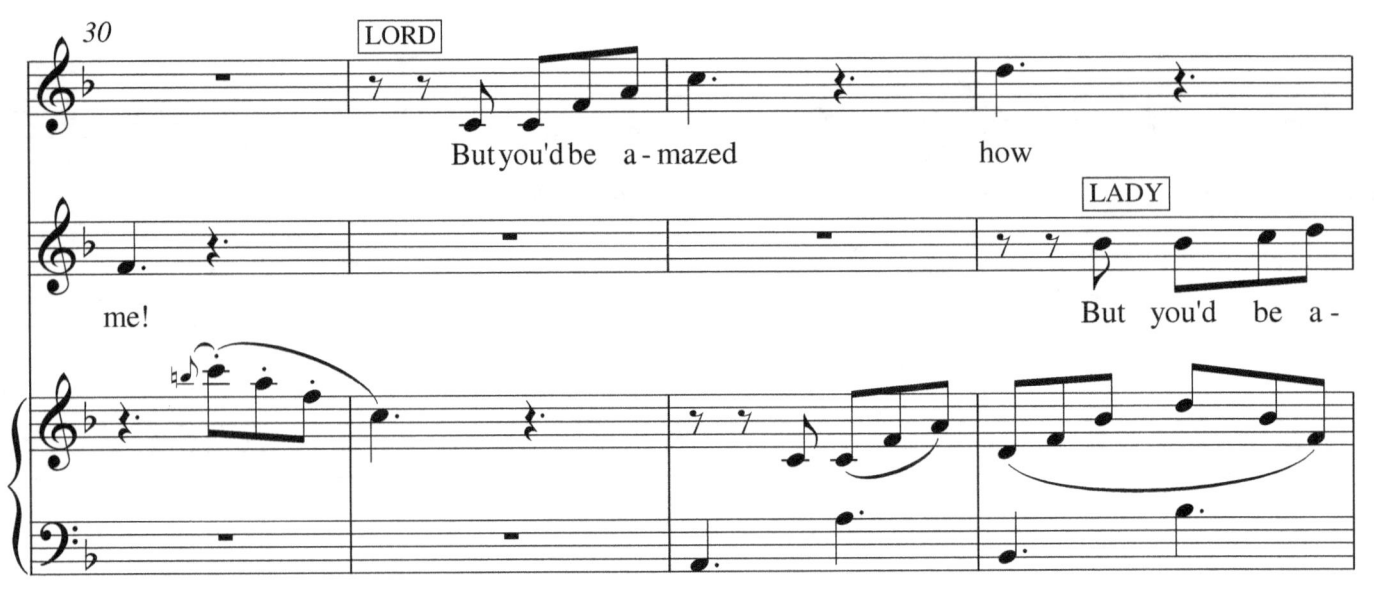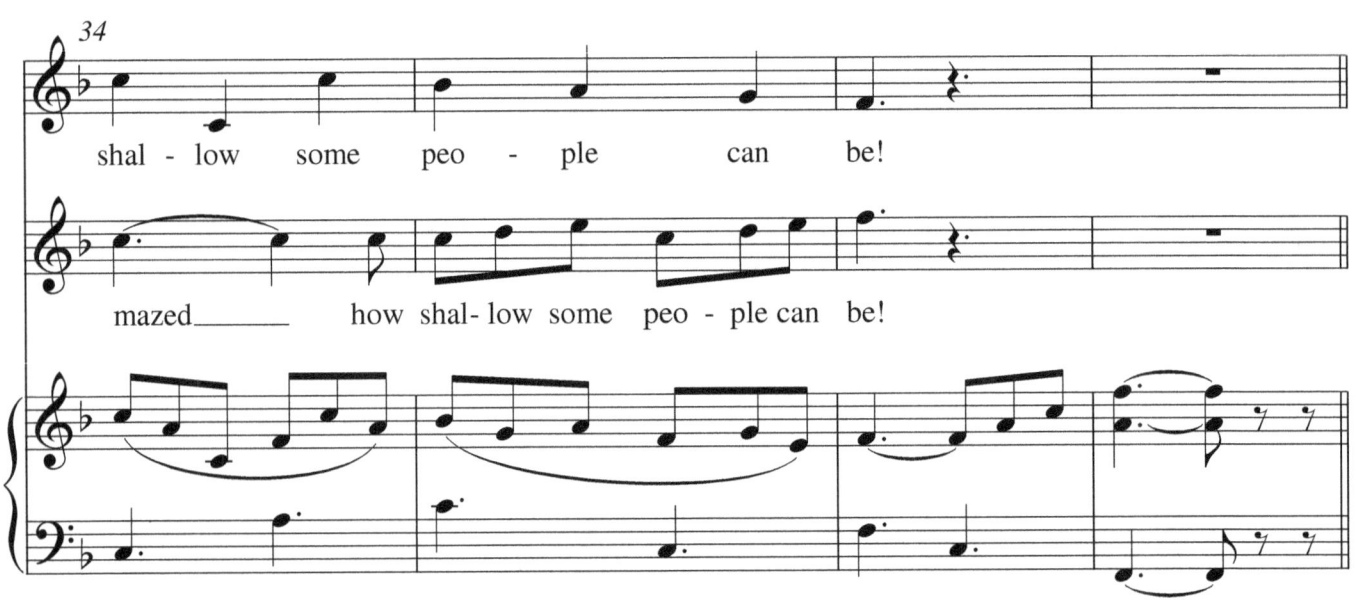

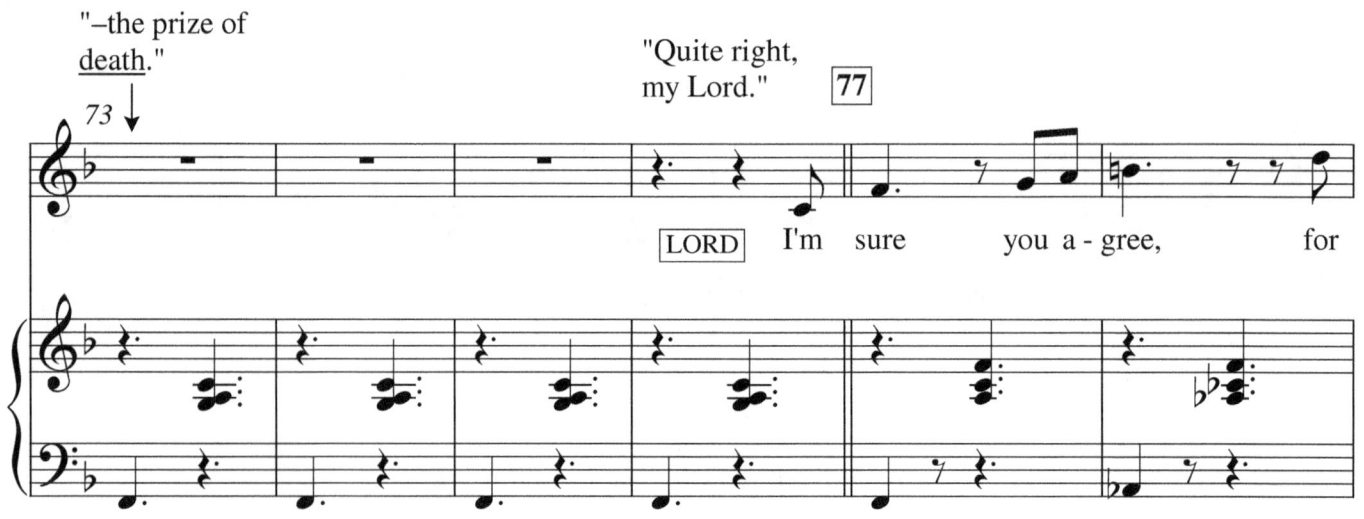

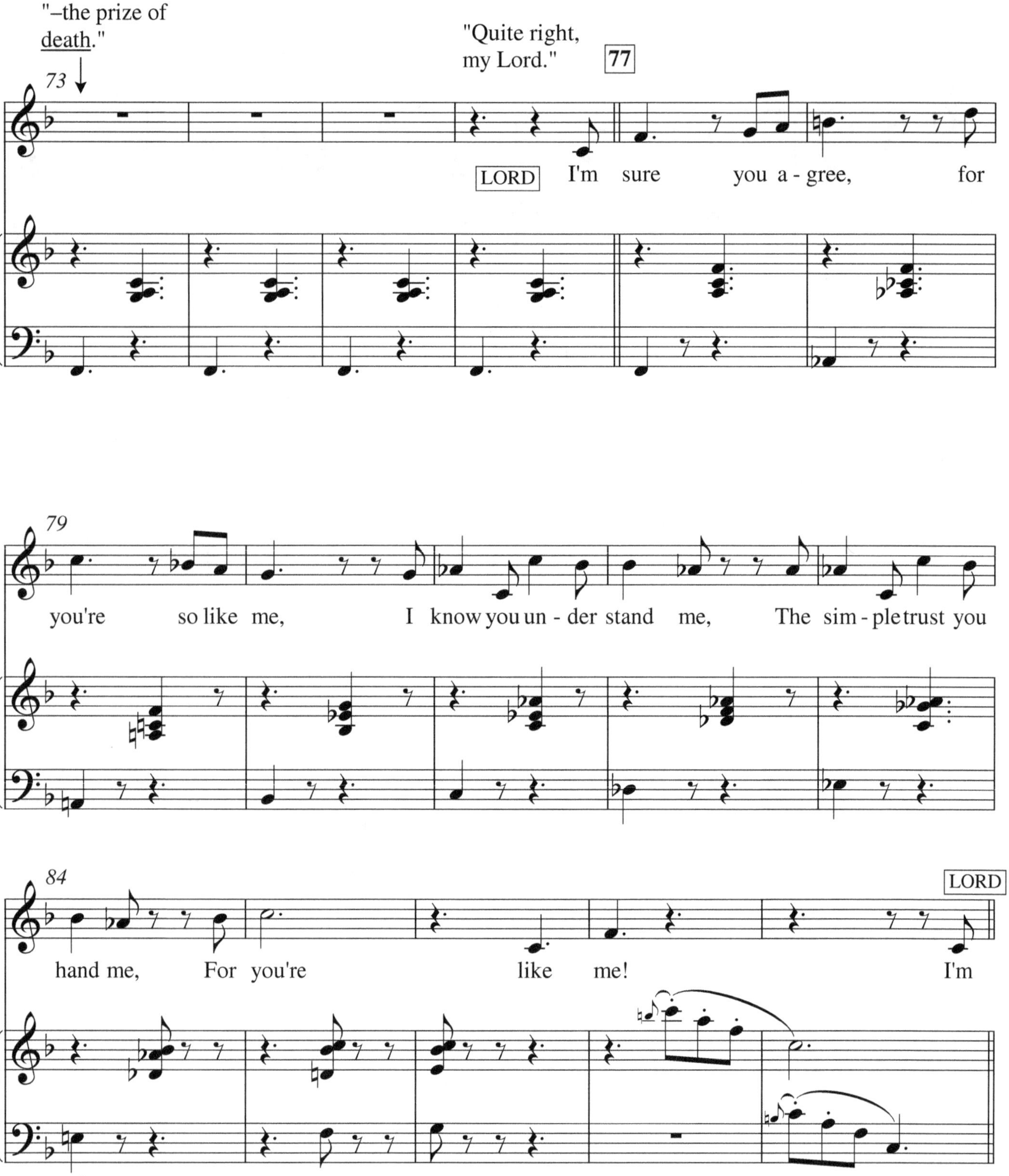
"–the prize of death."
"Quite right, my Lord."
77
73
LORD
I'm sure you a - gree, for
79
you're so like me, I know you un - der stand me, The sim - ple trust you
84
hand me, For you're like me!
LORD
I'm

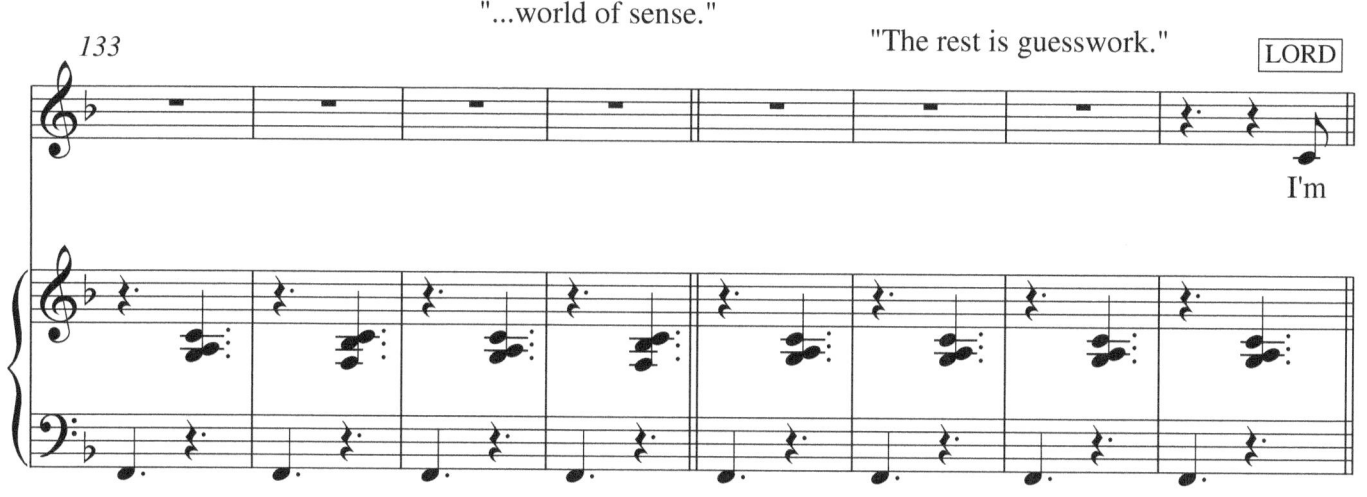

146
hind you. The an-gels have de-signed you, Yes, you're like me!
flute

152
153
LORD
I'm sure you a - gree, for you're so like
LADY
Oh, I a- gree, I a-gree, You'll nev-er know how I a-
MAN
I'm sure. my Lord, Oh yes, I a-
cello
Pno. play all

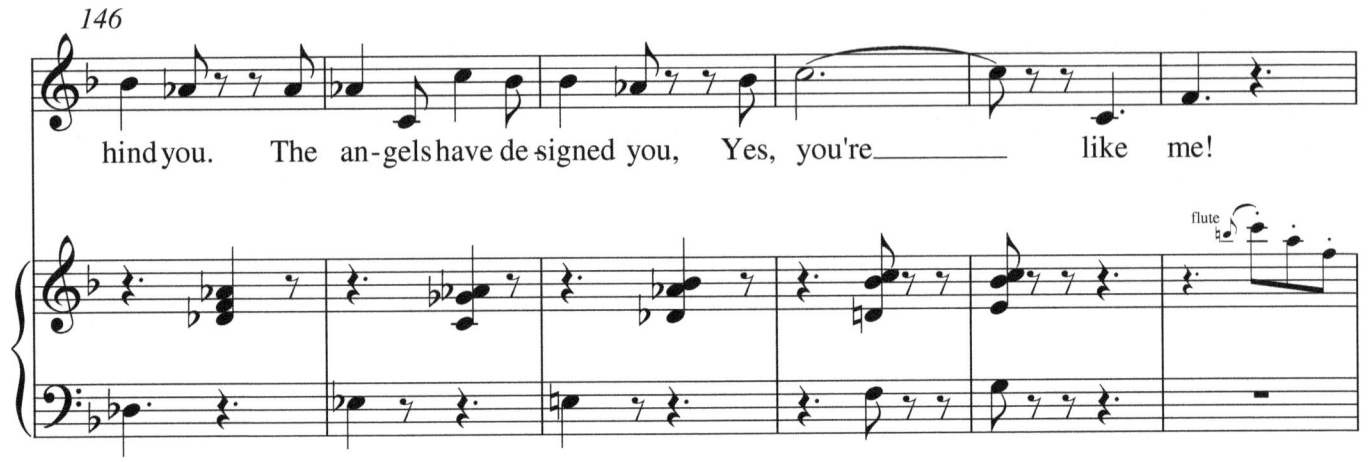

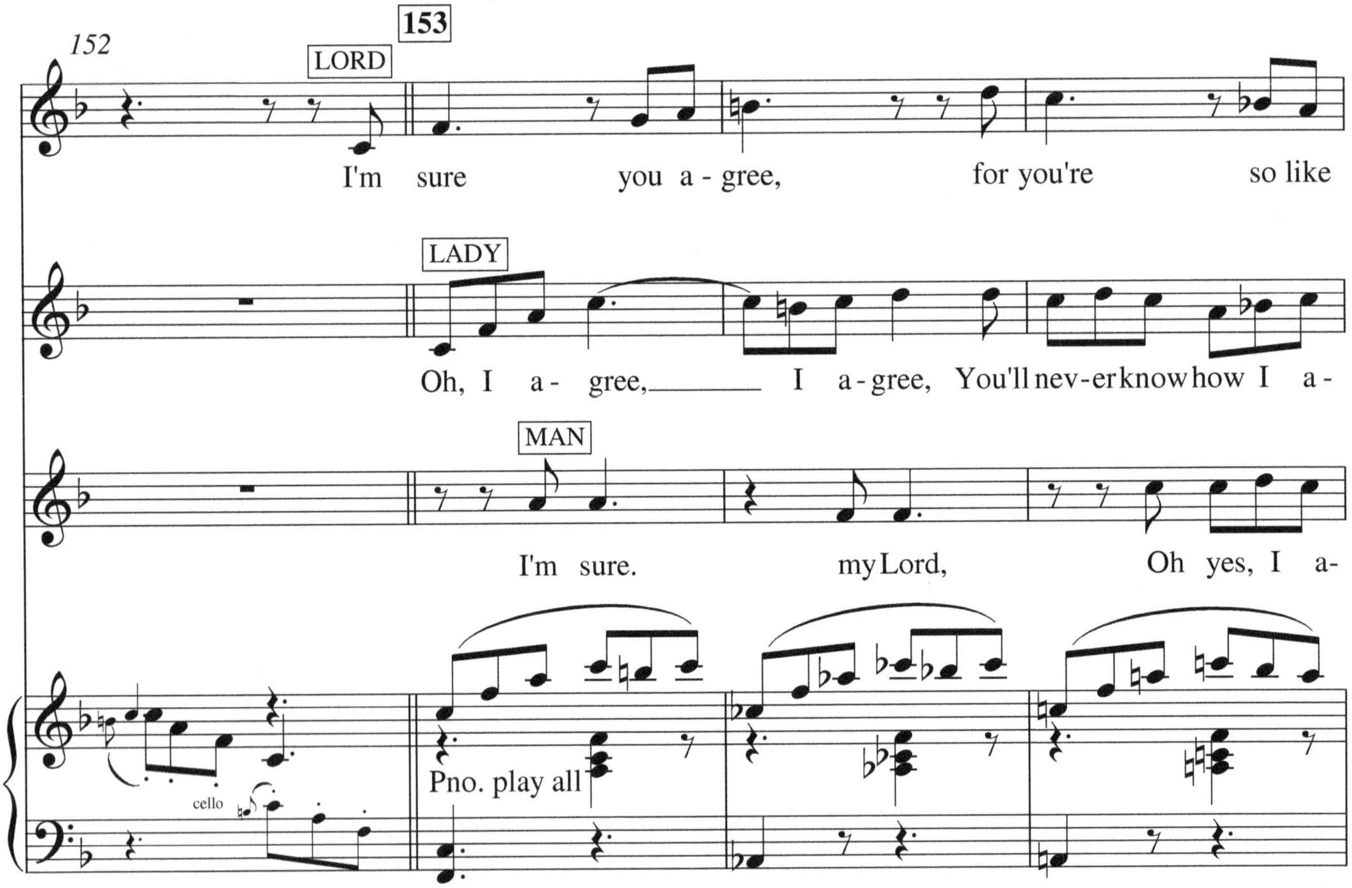

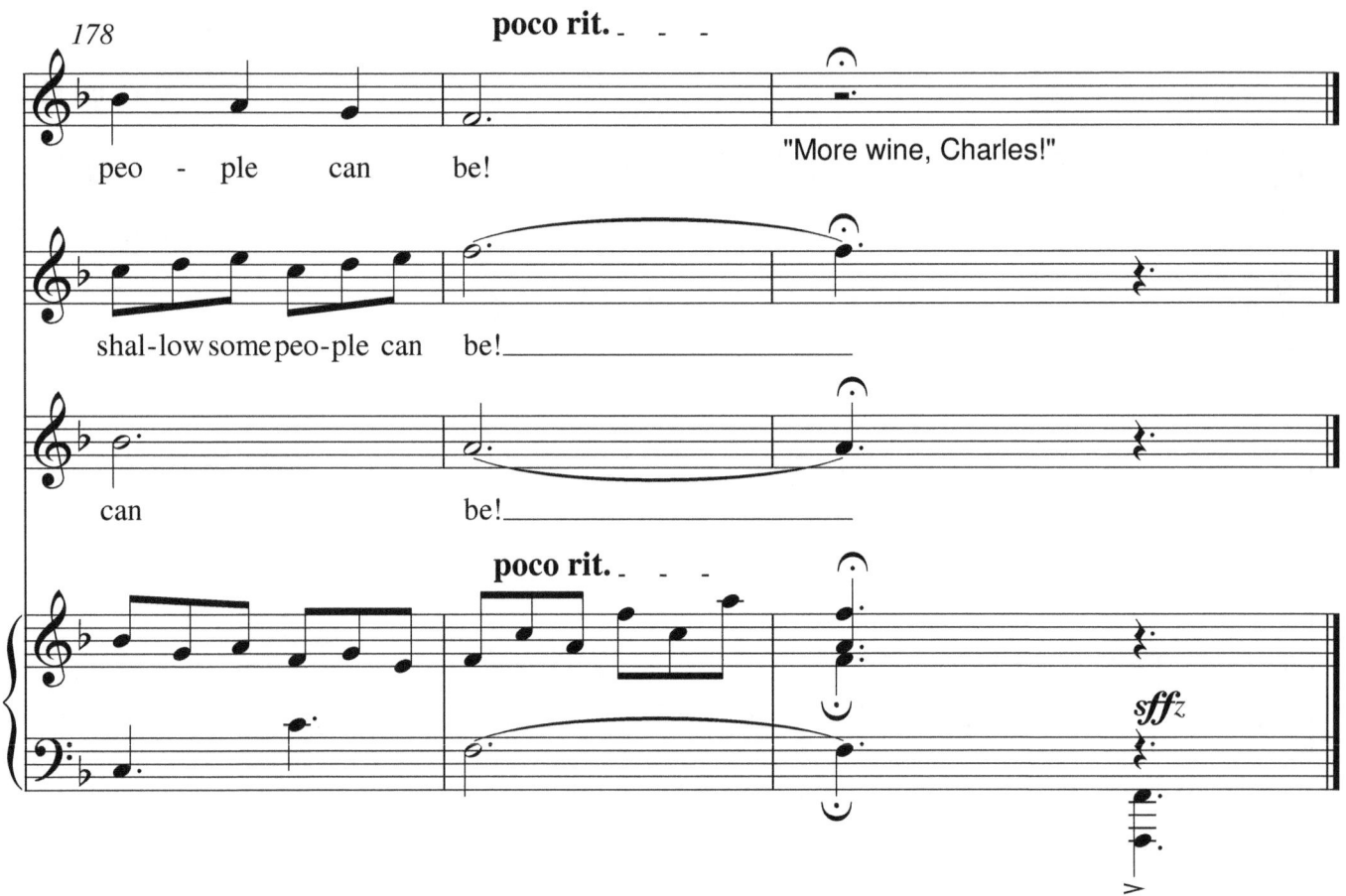

13 With A Friend Like You
[Lady, Lord]

WARN: "Set your mind at rest. We shall be undisturbed."

CUE (Lady): "Undisturbed?"

101

The Hour Is Late
(Wayside Inn Reprise)

[Lord]

15 Come To The Masquerade
[Man]

After Masquerade

15-A

CUE: Applause Segue from previous

15-B Masquerade Waltz #1

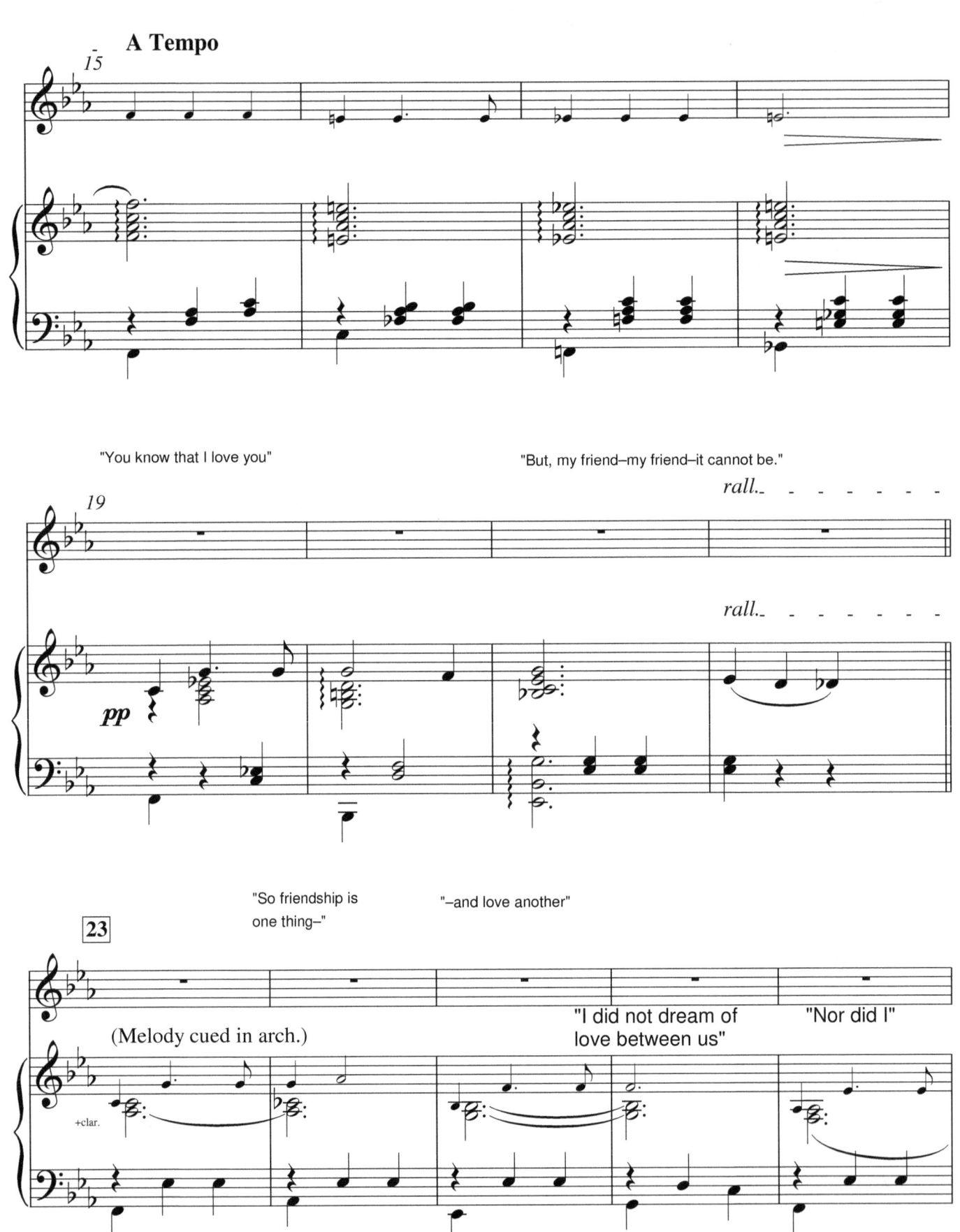

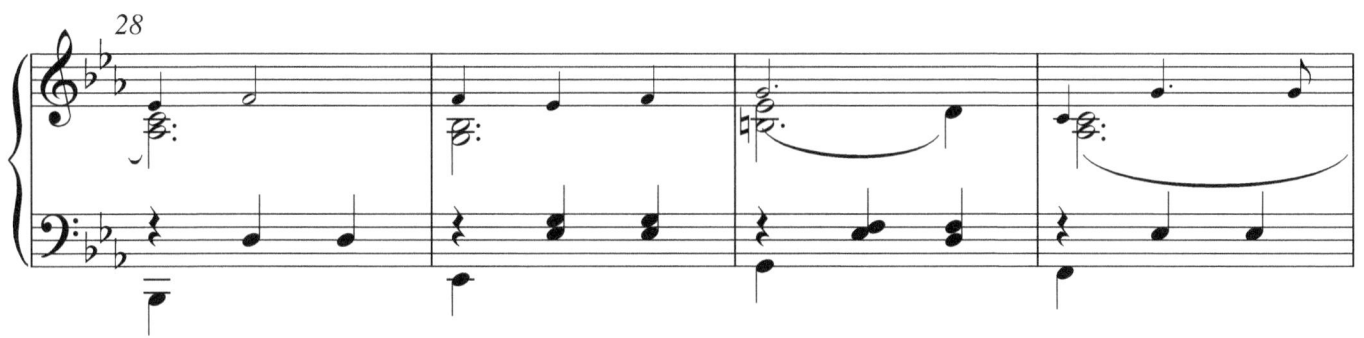

Masquerade Waltz #2

15-C

SEGUE AS ONE

16 Man With A Load Of Mischief

[The Lady]

CUE: (Lady) "Too many arms have held me since then"

Freely

Vocal: A man can say "I love you" and swear a sol-emn vow, But then you find he's mere-ly A man with a load of mis-chief; A

Keyboard: 'cello (Orch.)

Tempo Moderato

♩=72

man can say "for-ev-er" but all you know is now; As time goes by he's

119

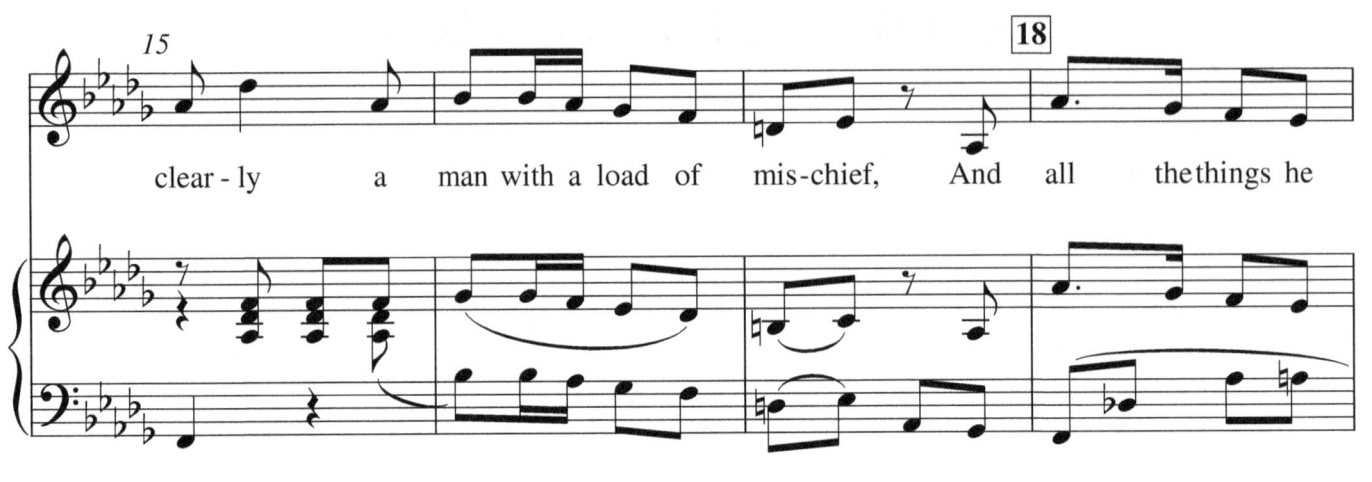

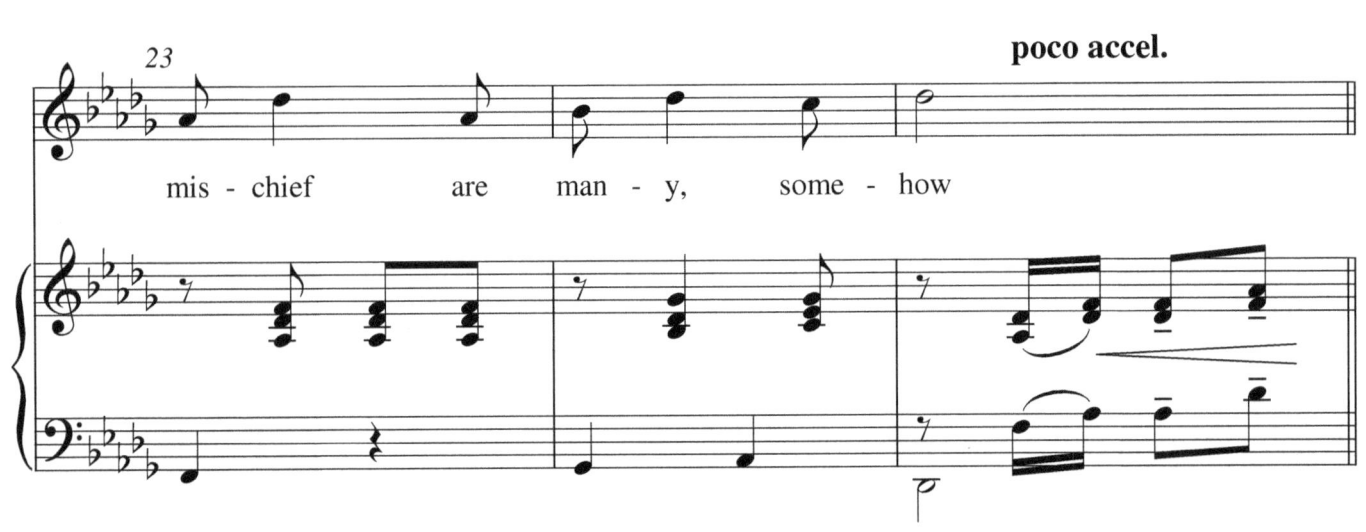

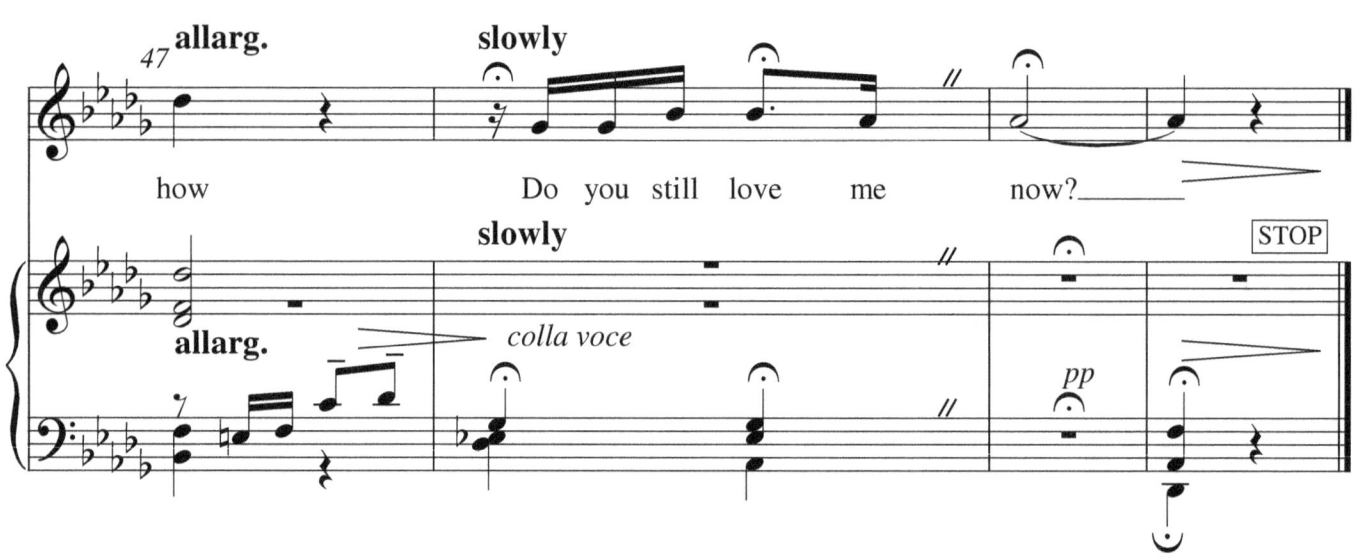

Ending Reprise

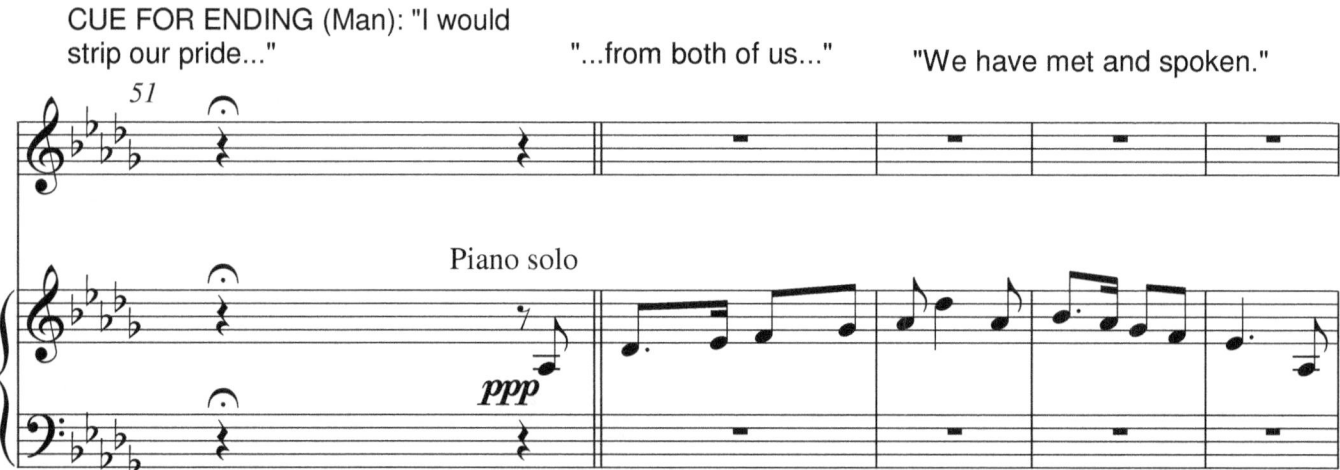

"forget" "beg" "You will give what is in your heart.""
56
LADY
tutti
+clar.
p
+cello
And all the things he tells you you're
62
a tempo
long - ing to be - lieve in, But men with loads of
Lady: "Who are you..."
65
mis - chief are man - y some - how
SEGUE ON CUE: "World of stratagem" (kiss)

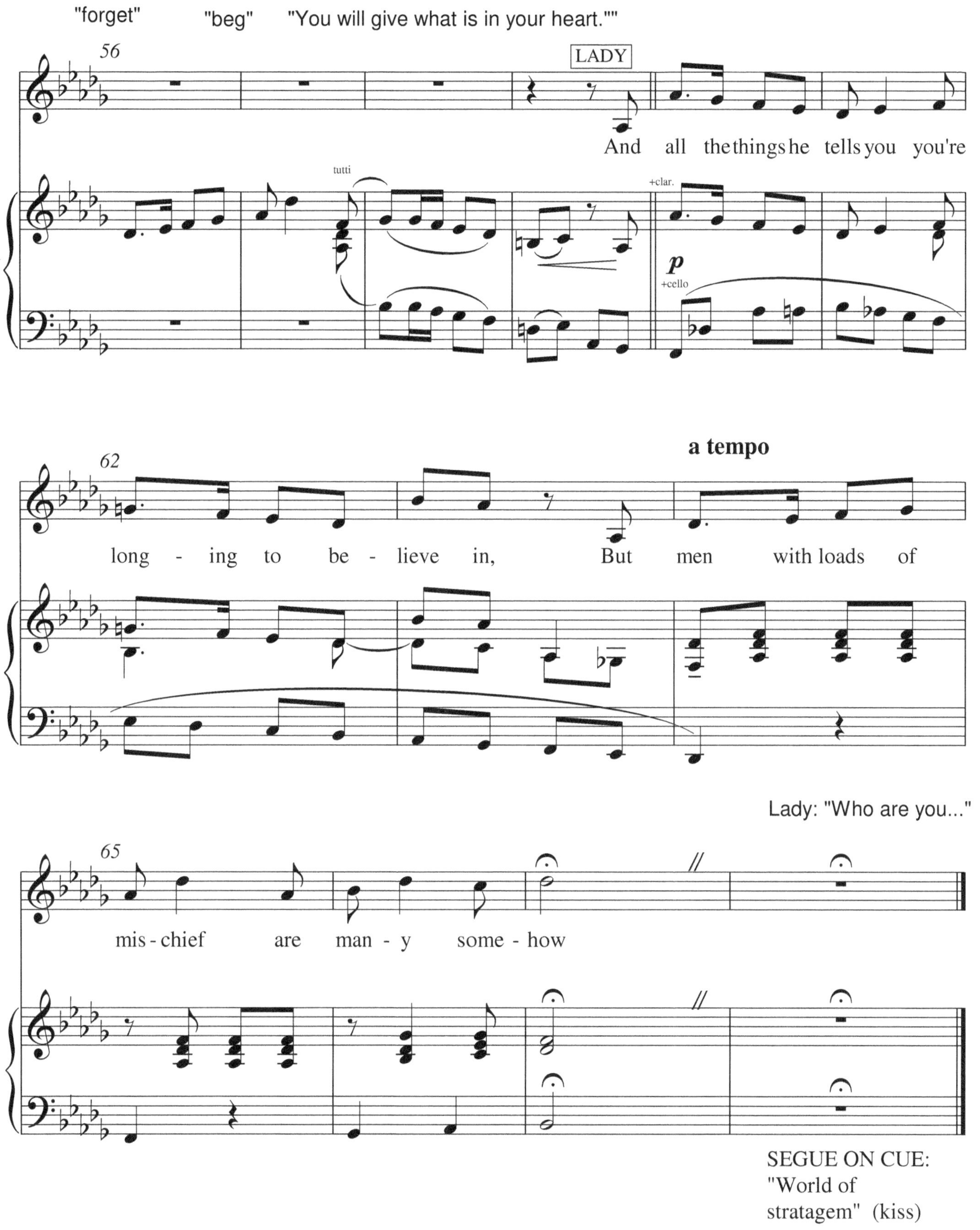

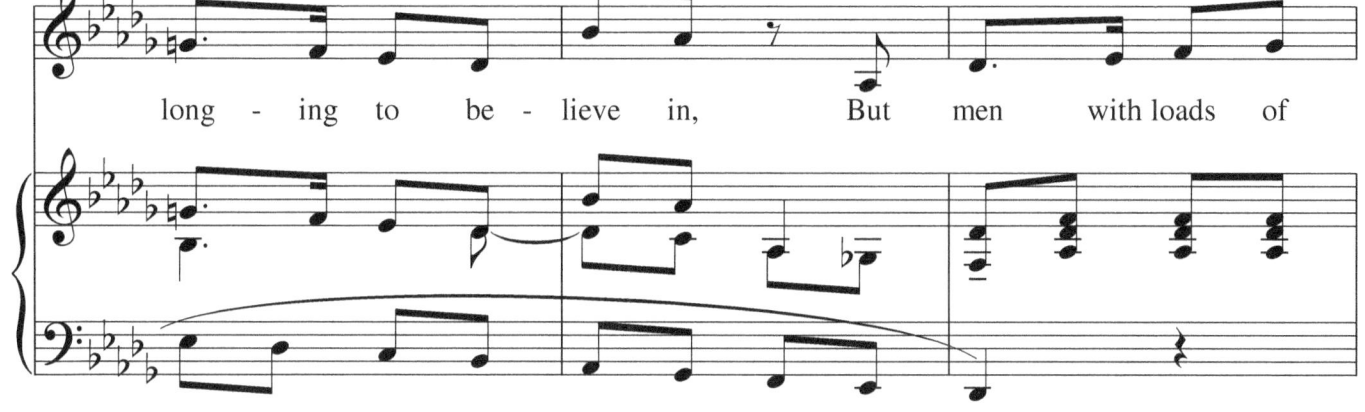

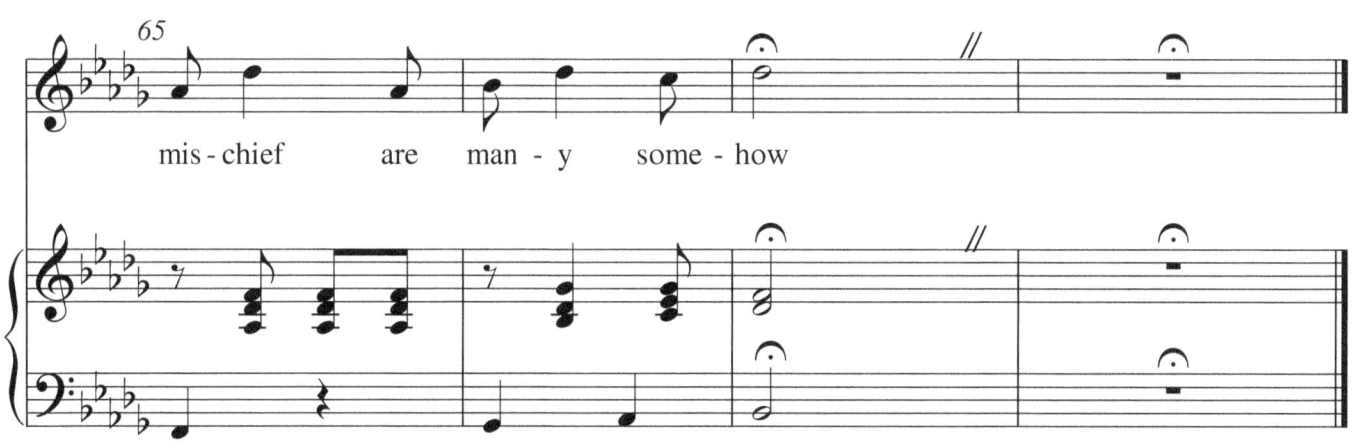

Masquerade Reprise Intro

16-A

124

Masquerade (Reprise)

CUE: segue from previous

[Man]

♩ = 104
Moderato

The music is playing, the moments go by, And I hear the same serenade The

What Style!

[Innkeeper]

10 Relaxed Waltz
ser - vants and maids might dab - ble a - while, but nob - les and la - dies,
+cello
16
they've got the style! Oh, just im - ag - ine how it must have been– The lov - li - est af - fair you've
flute
(Pno. tacet)
cello
21
23 Più mosso
ev - er seen He draws the shut - ters tight; The moon is out of sight, The
(Play)
p

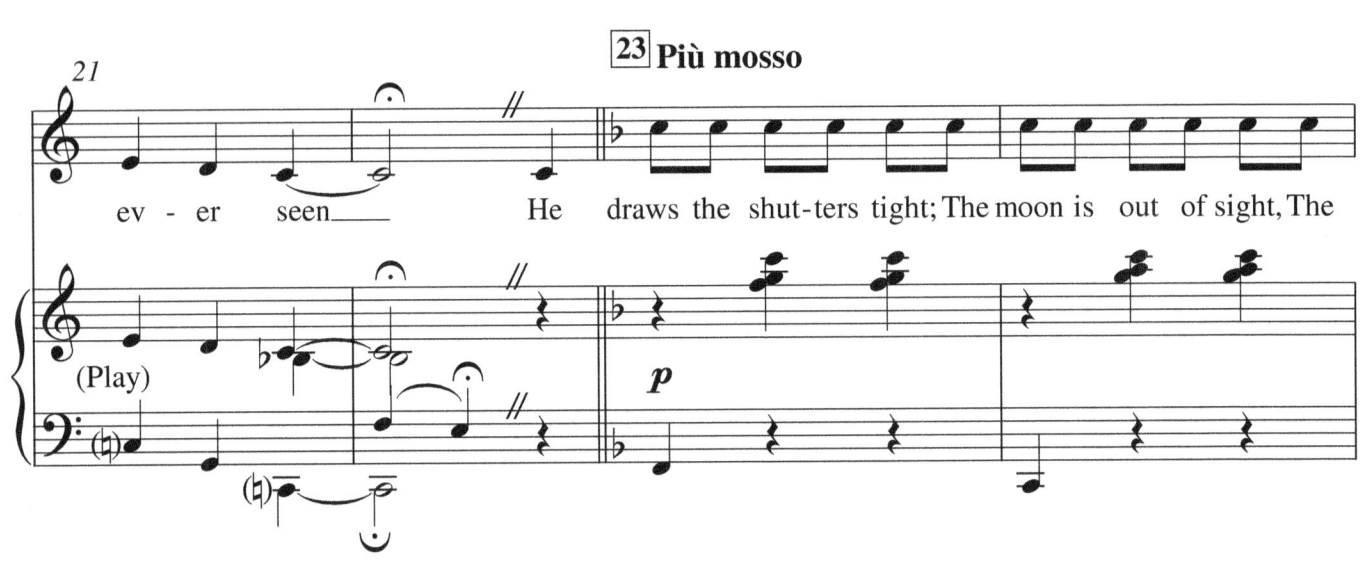

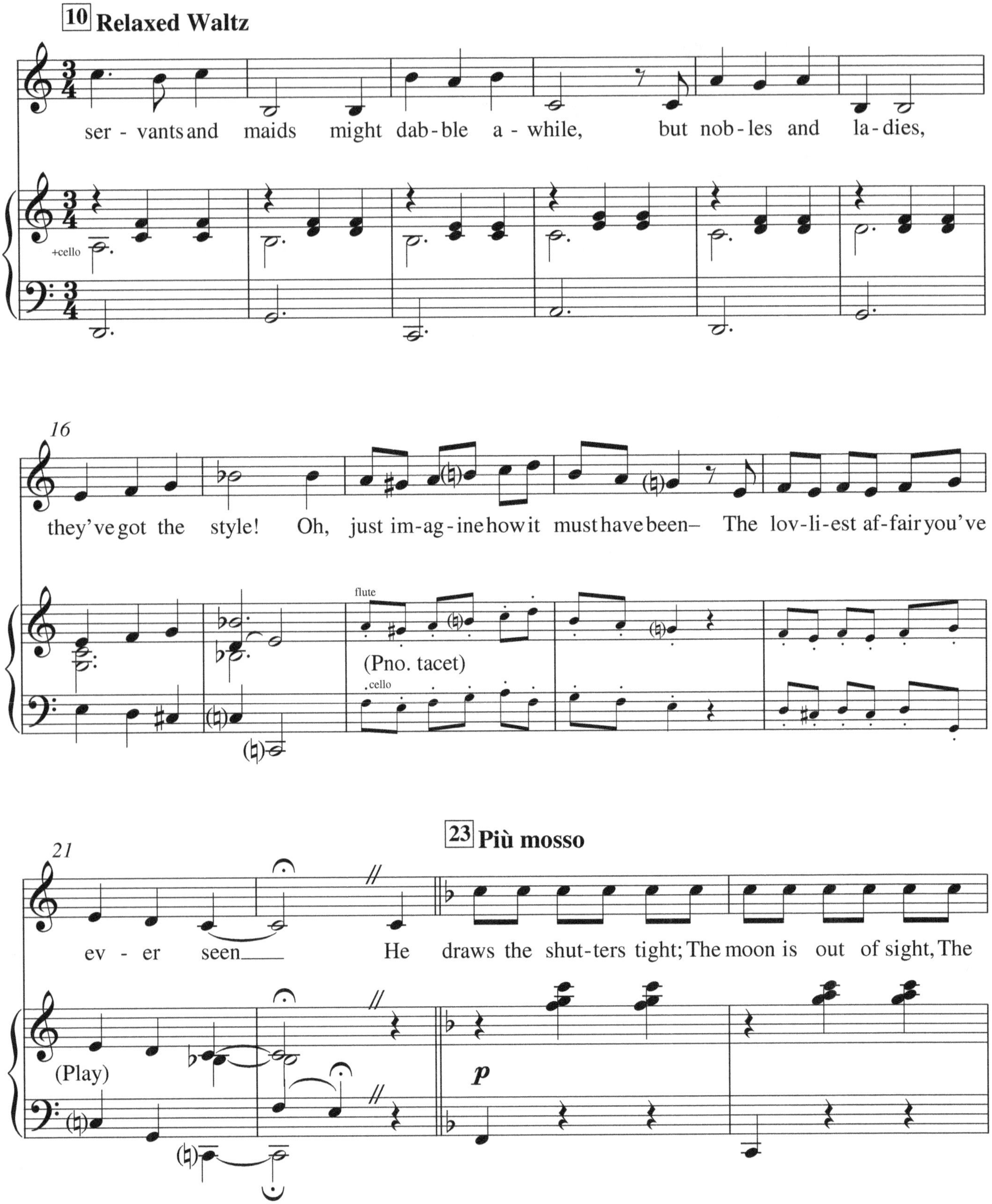

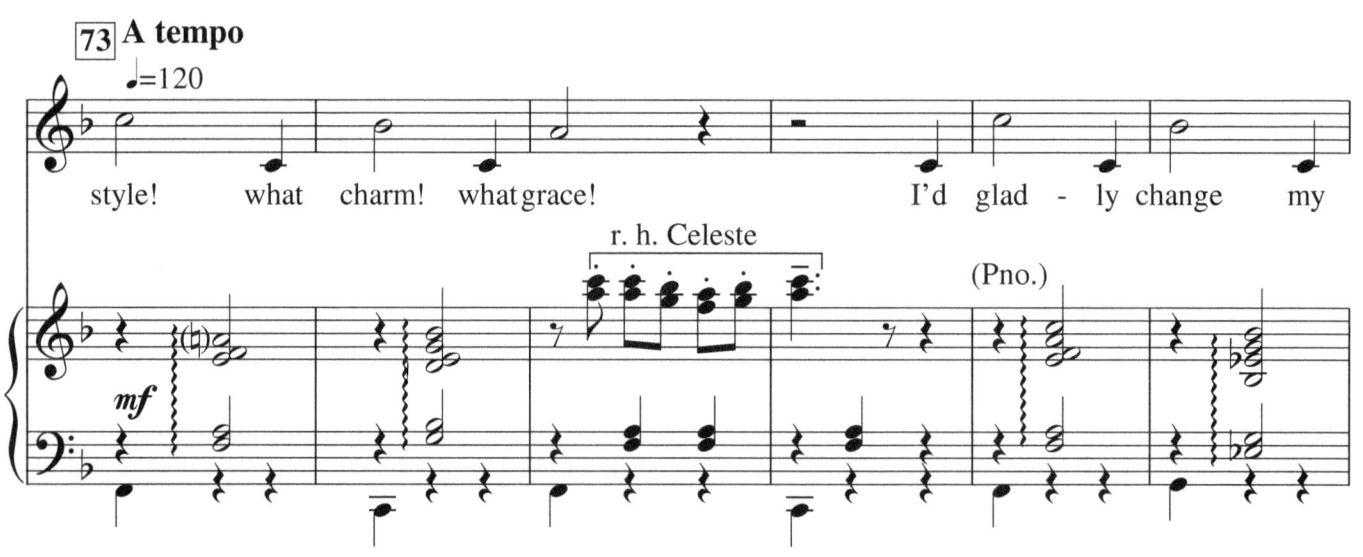

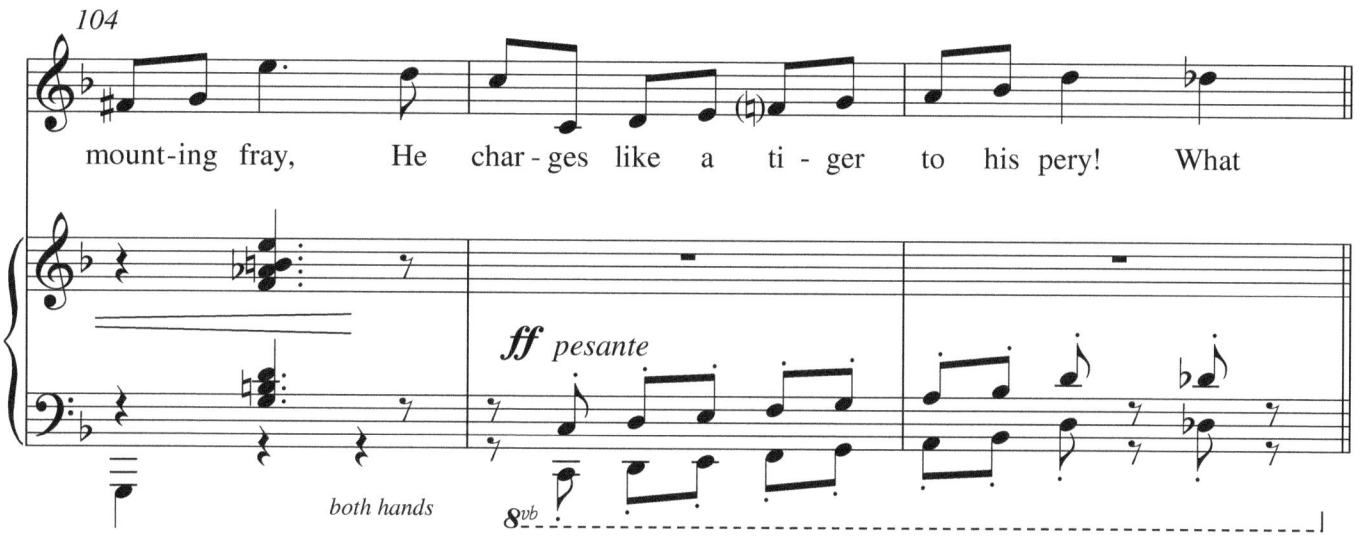

"...change my place— I'm not sure I could keep up with the pace."

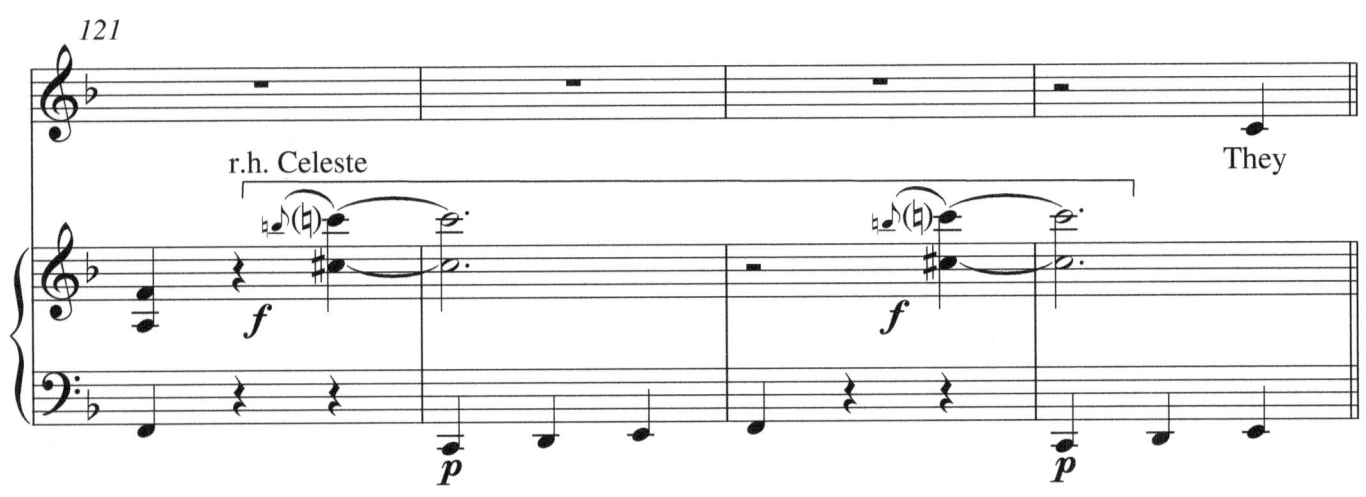

They

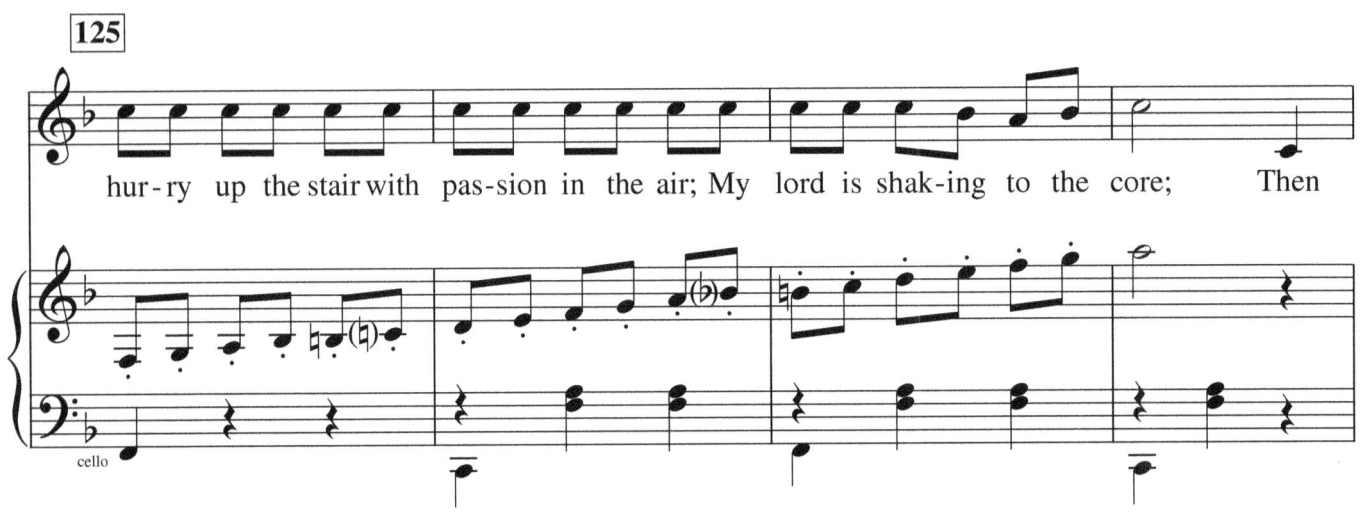

hur-ry up the stair with pas-sion in the air; My lord is shak-ing to the core;   Then

138

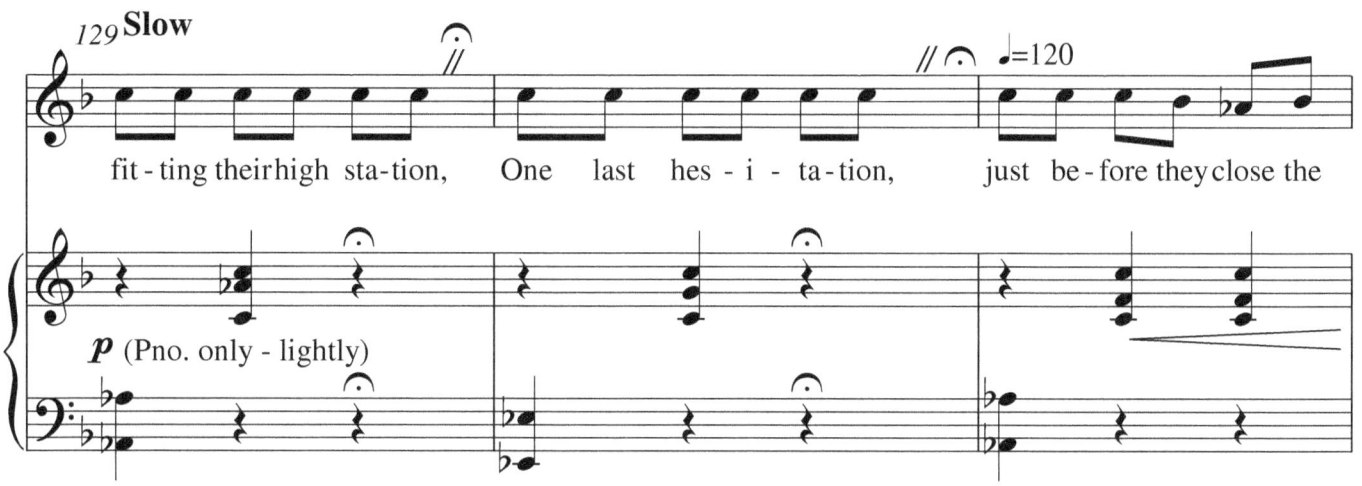

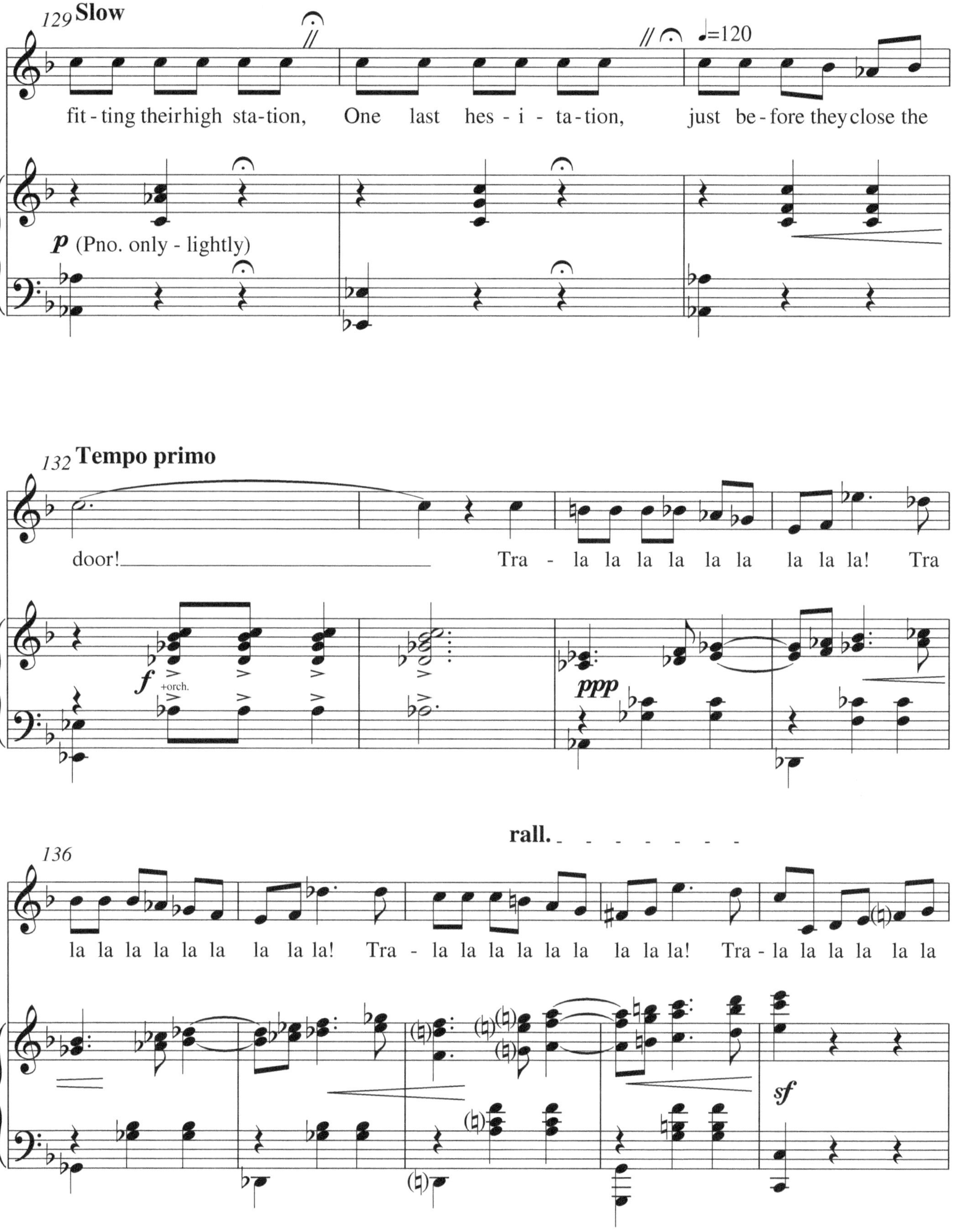
129 Slow
♩=120
fit-ting their high sta-tion, One last hes-i-ta-tion, just be-fore they close the
p (Pno. only - lightly)
132 Tempo primo
door! Tra-la la la la la la la la la! Tra
f +orch.
ppp
136
rall.
la la la la la la la la la! Tra-la la la la la la la la la! Tra-la la la la la la
sf

19-A

"What Style!" Fragment
[Innkeeper]

WARN: "–tell a tale if he wished."

CUE (Wife): "–chance for a good profit."

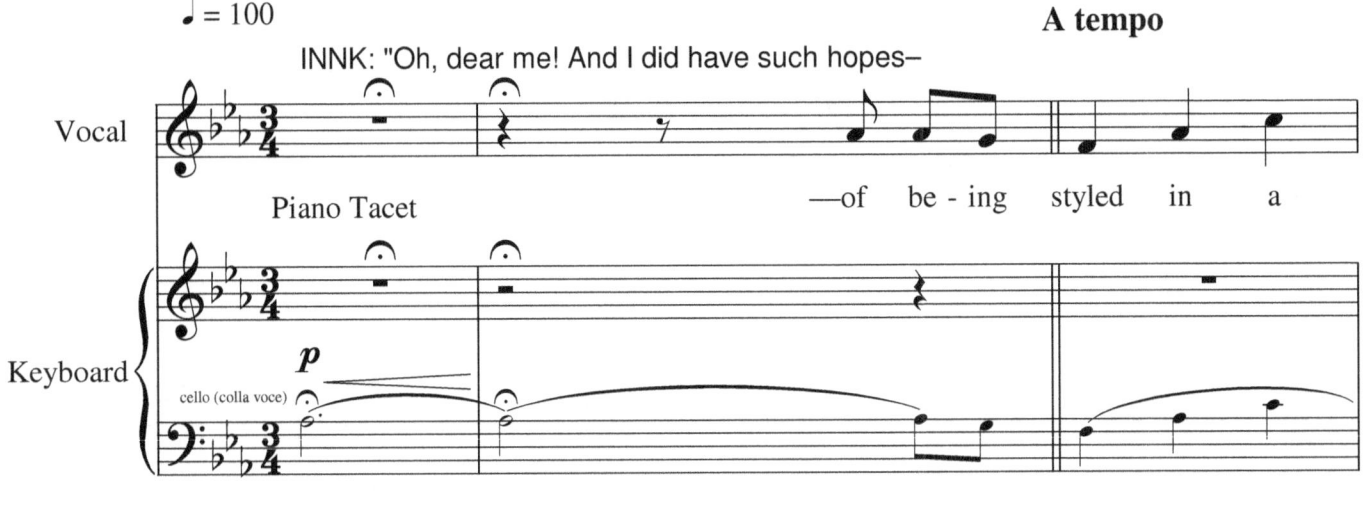

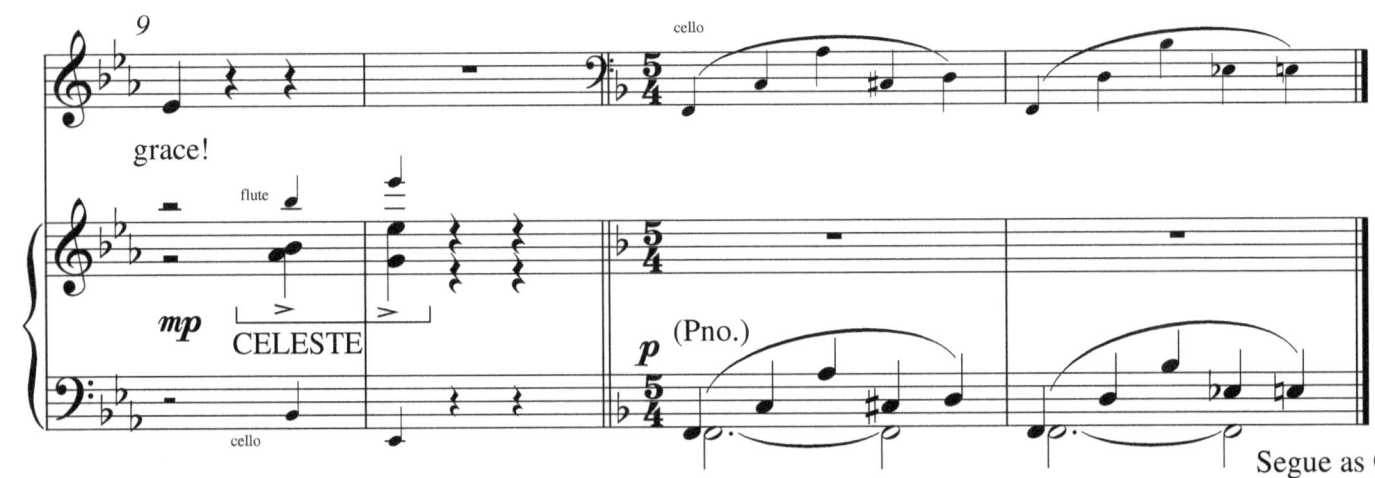

Segue as O

A Wonder

[Lady]

CUE: Segue from previous

143

Make Way For My Lady

[Man]

CUE (Lady): "Then I leave you with it."

148

Make Way Playoff

21-A

SIGHT CUE: Man turns upstage.

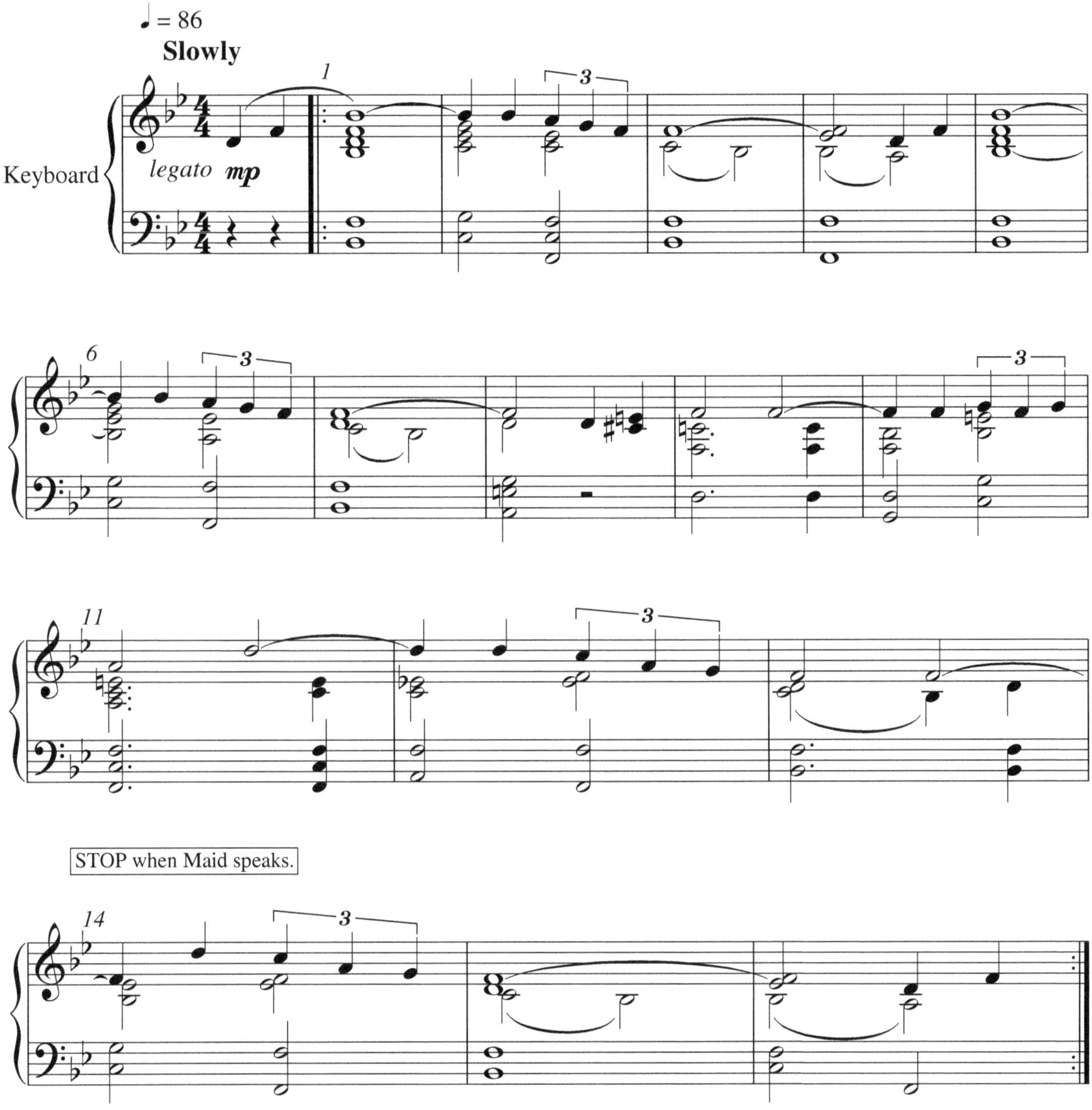

♩ = 86
Slowly

legato **mp**

STOP when Maid speaks.

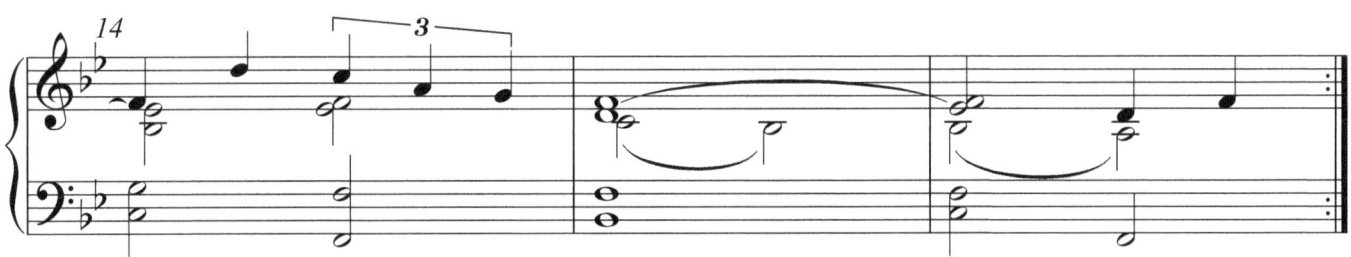

22 Forget!

[Lord]

CUE (Maid): "I was thinking about you."

Forget Reprise
[Lord]

CUE (Lord): One of us at least upholds the banner of chastity—"

Any Other Way
[Wife, Innkeeper]

CUE (Wife): "As usual!"

159

Before Rag Doll

[Maid]

CUE (Lady): "Bring my cloak when I call, Louise." [Lady exits]

Note: Cuts are sometimes made in this number. On the cast album version, the following measures were CUT: 13-18, 23-25.

Little Rag Doll

[Maid]

24-A

CUE: Direct segue from previous

24-B

After Rag Doll

[Scene Change]

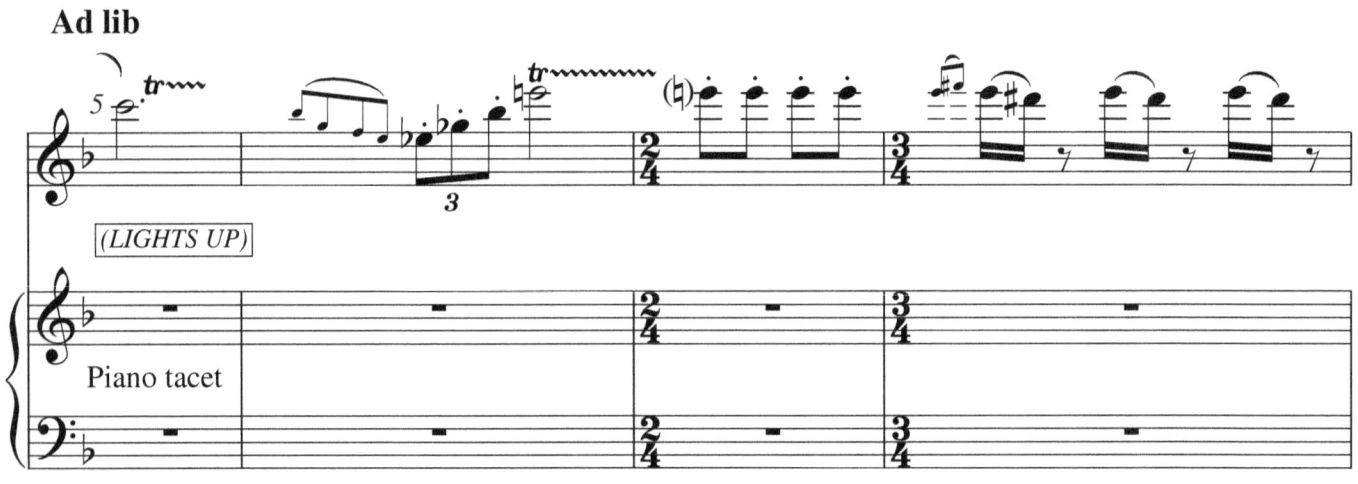

170

Romance [Reprise]

[Lady, Lord]

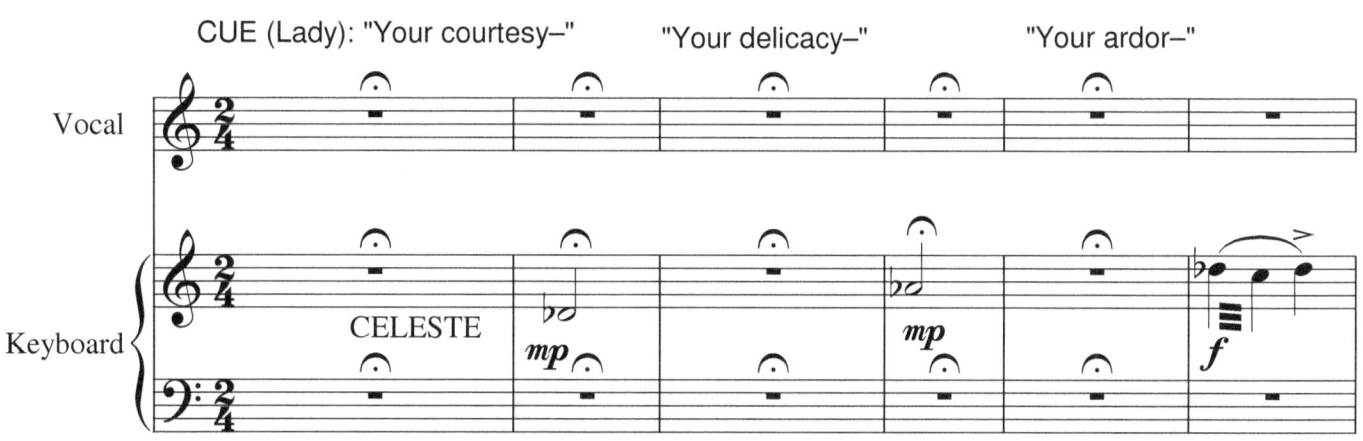

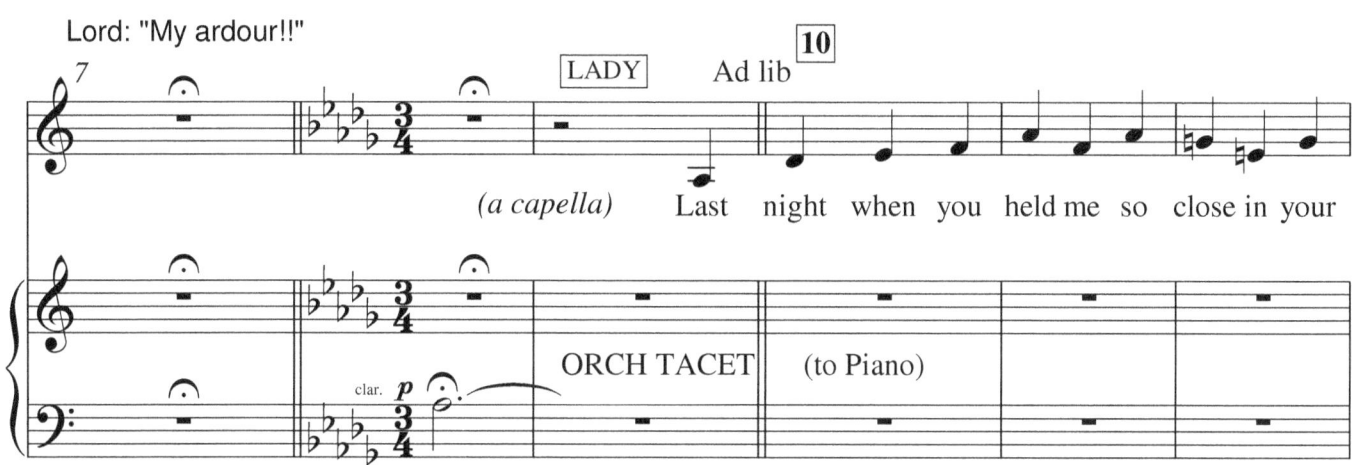

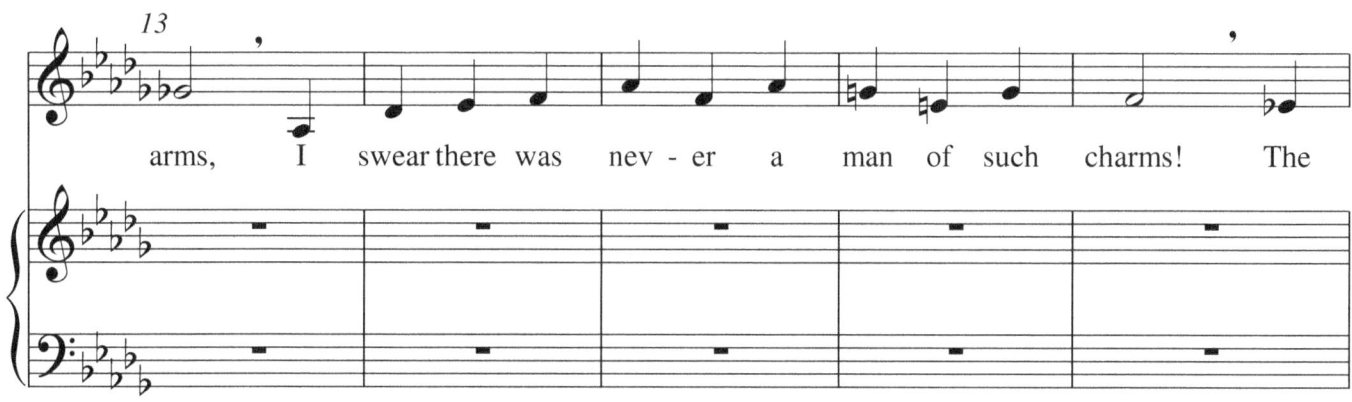

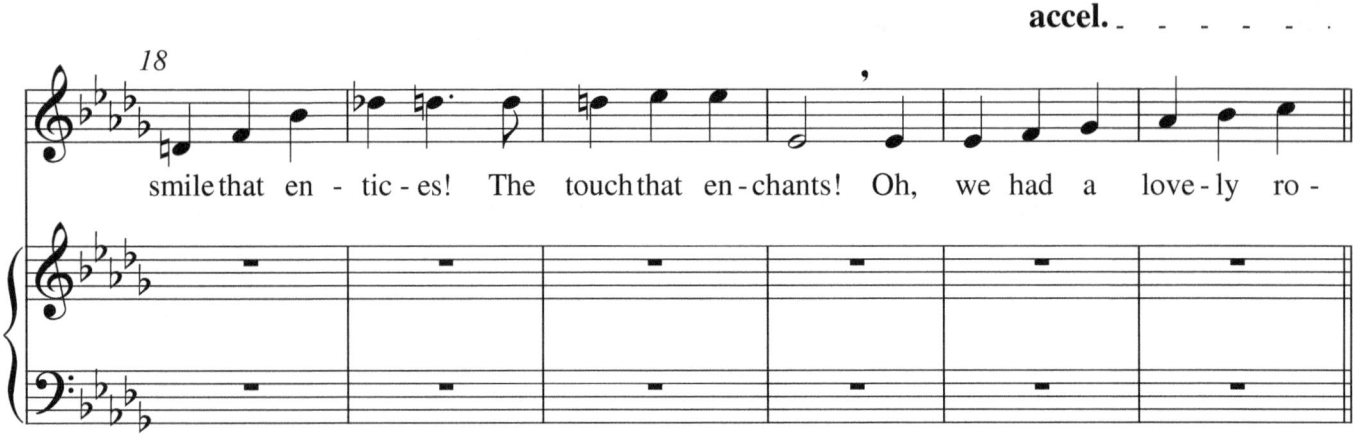
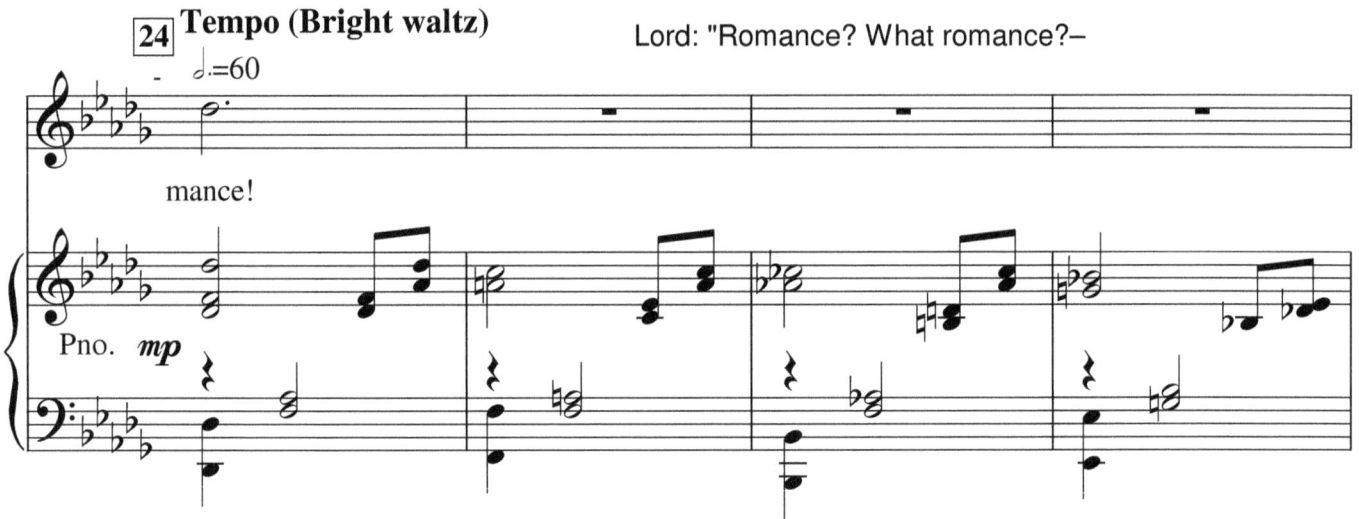
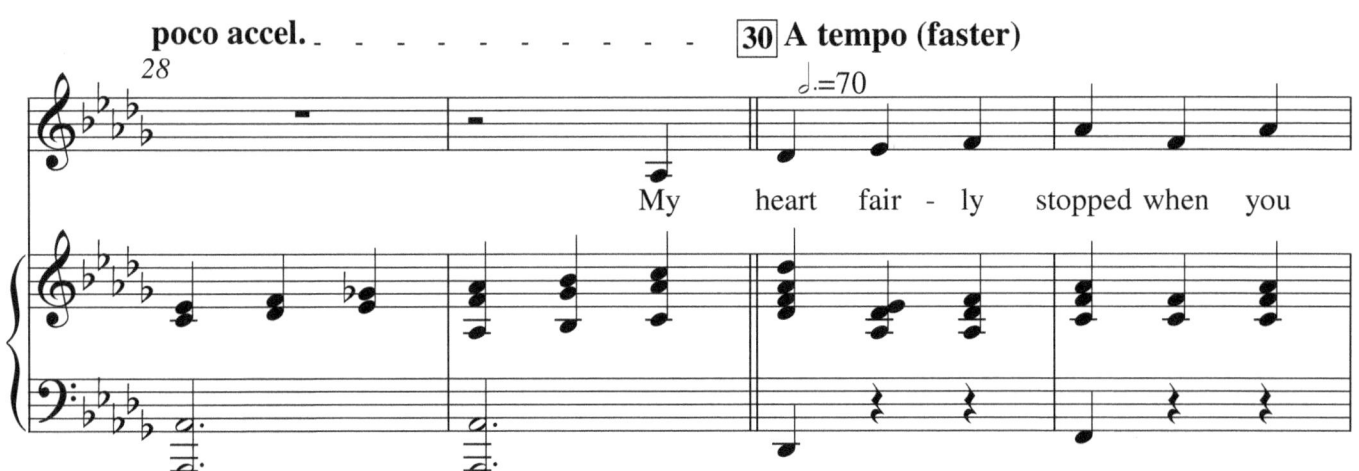

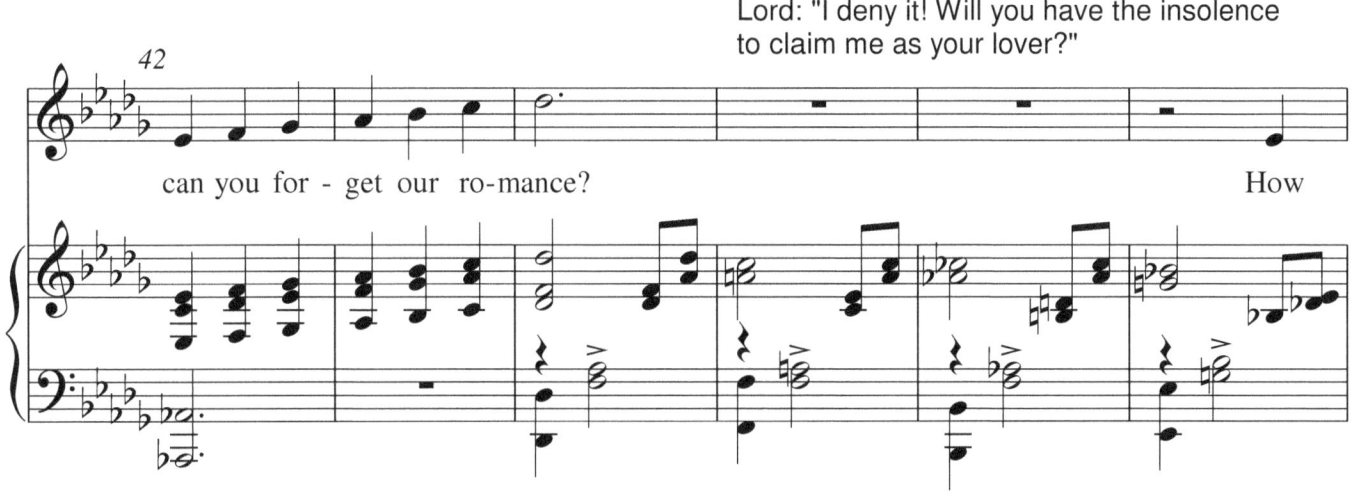

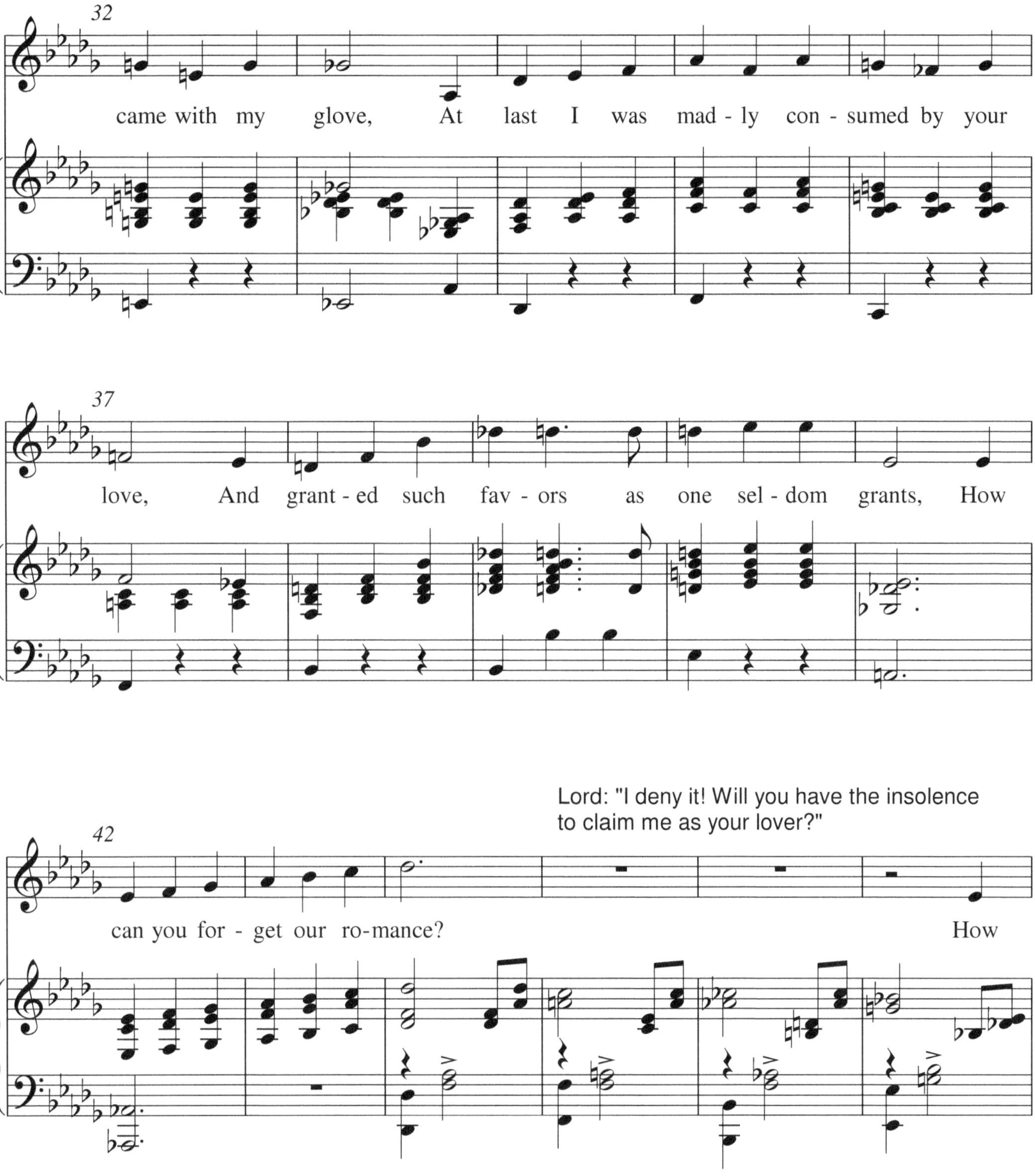
32
came with my glove, At last I was mad - ly con - sumed by your
37
love, And grant - ed such fav - ors as one sel - dom grants, How
Lord: "I deny it! Will you have the insolence
to claim me as your lover?"
42
can you for - get our ro-mance? How

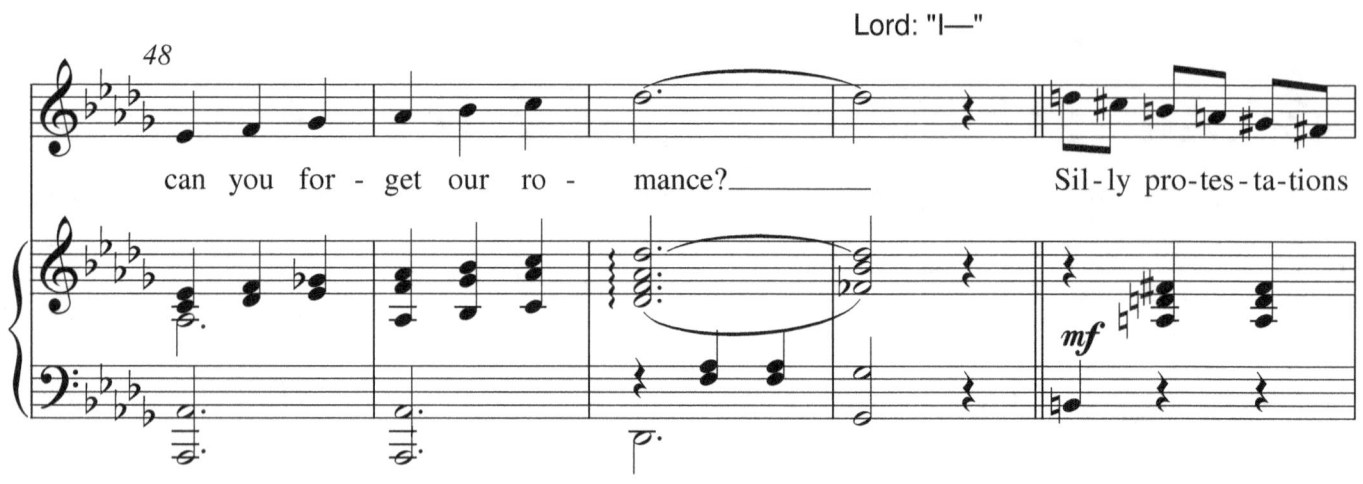

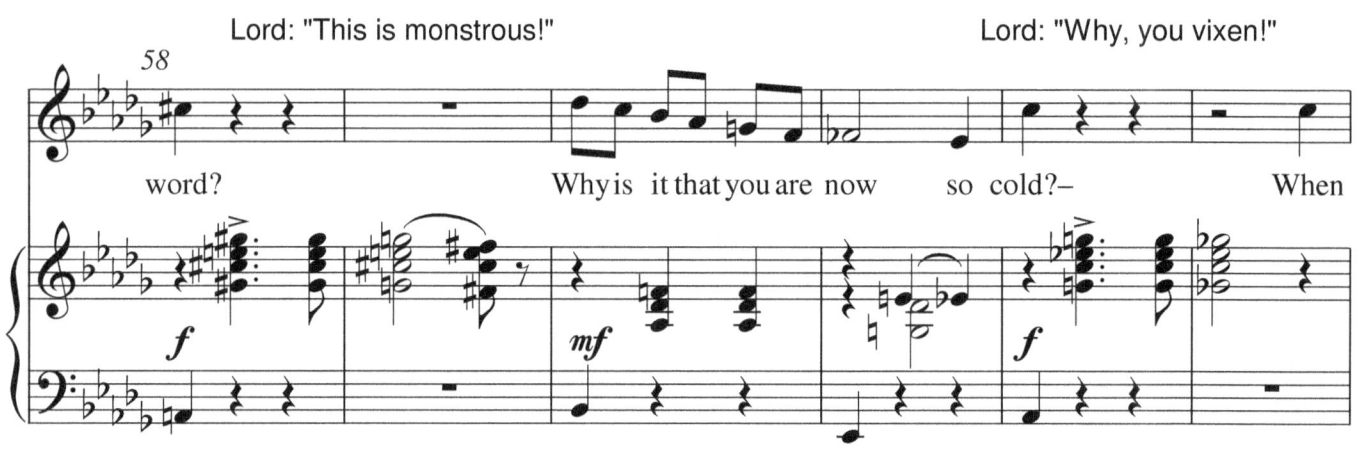

Man With A Load Of Mischief - Reprise

25-B

[Lady]

CUE (Man): "Fate plays peculiar tricks, my lady."
(Lady): "No, I think it is you who have been playing the tricks."

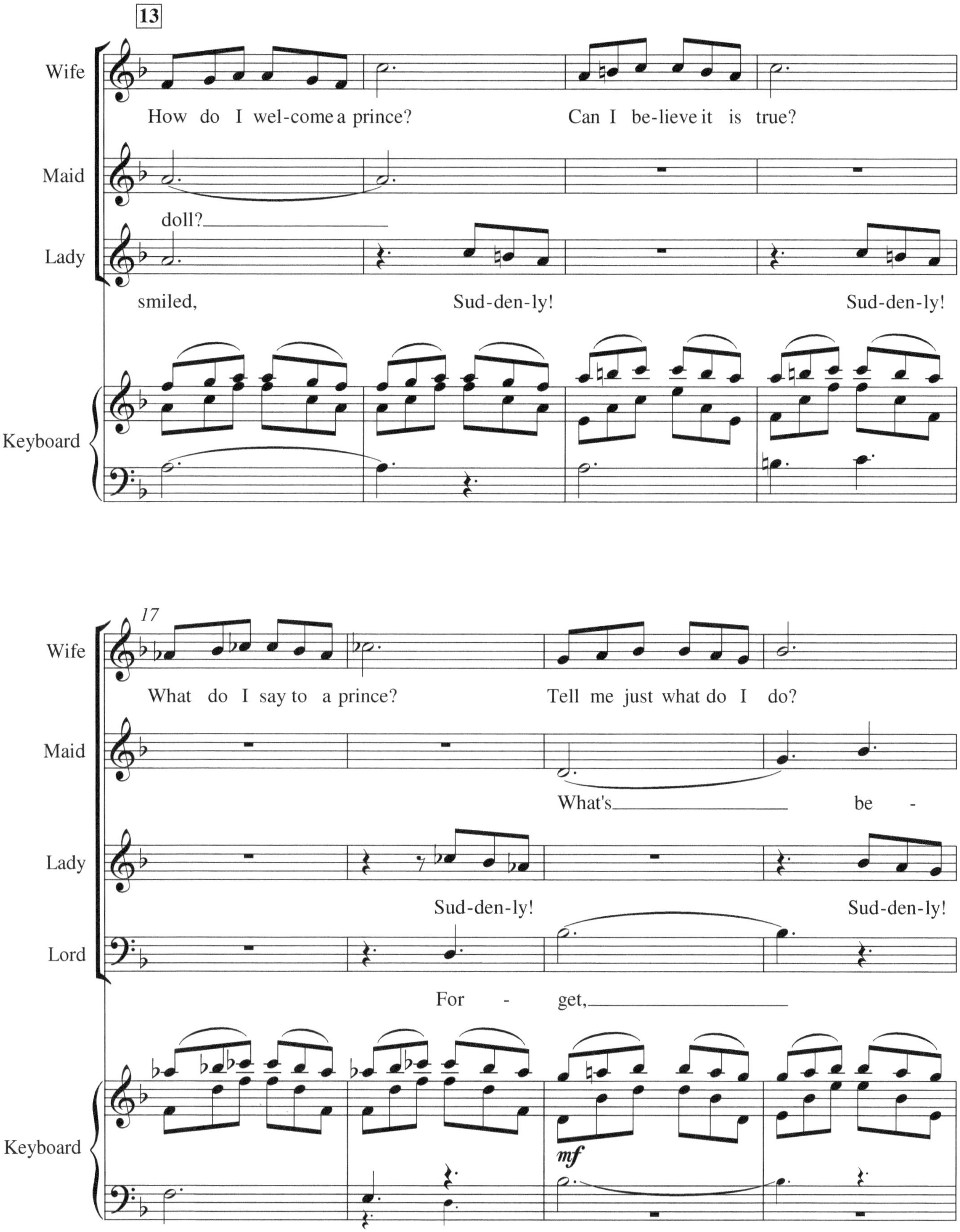

ALMOST SEGUE

Make Way - Reprise
[Man, Lady, Innkeeper, Wife]

27

CUE (Lord): "I forgot! Money–you'll need money!"

Lady: "I will stay! I can face the prince...

...Somehow with you I have no fear of the prospect."

Man: Louise, bring your lady's cloak."

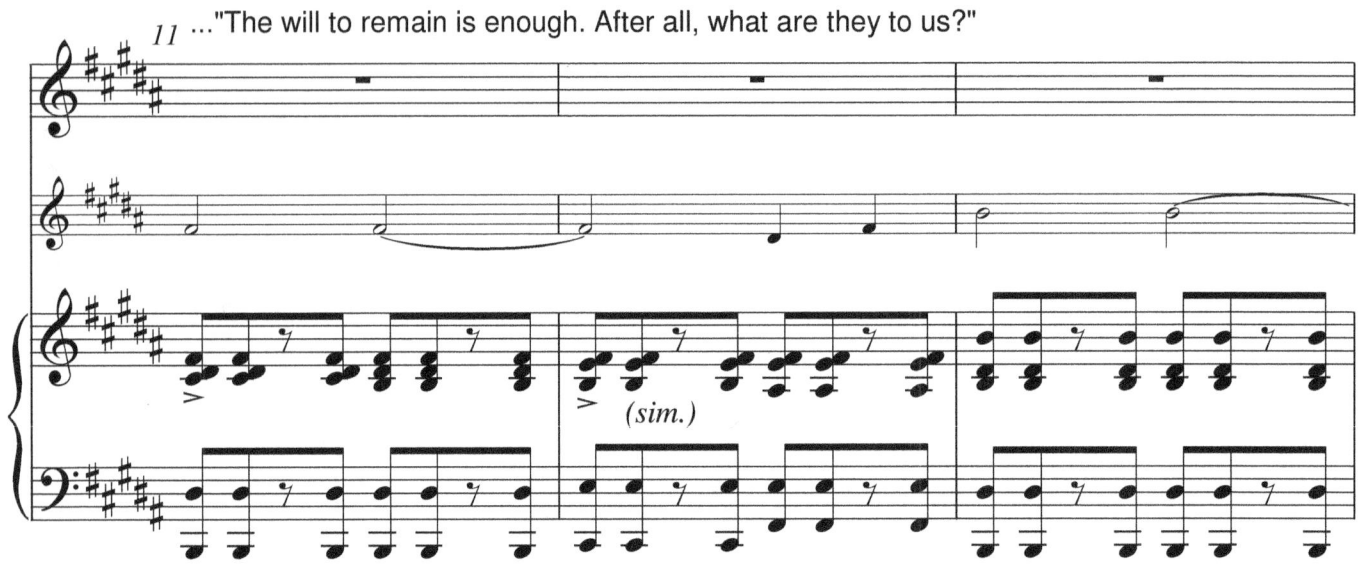

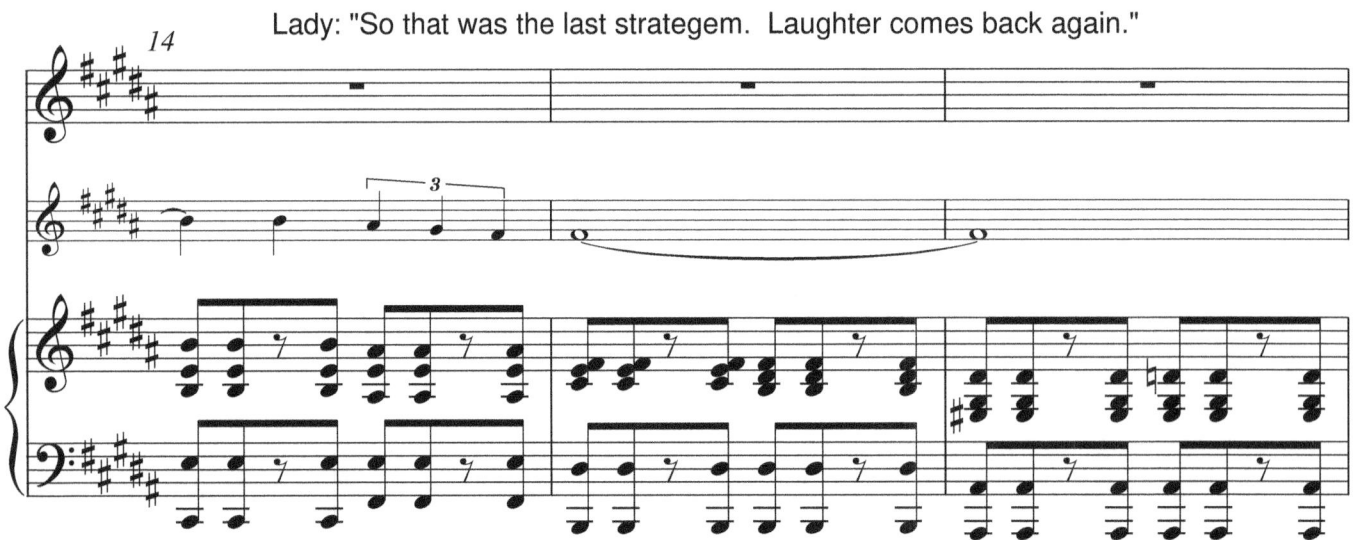

27-A

Coach Underscore

CUE: Segue from previous with no break

190

WARN for COACH HORN (Wife): "Laughing. Oh, how I love a daring romance!"

CUE for COACH HORN FX (Lord) "How dare they laugh!" [*See note]

* Note: In lieu of recorded sound effect, Piano play horn effect loco:
Tacet regular part on cue, play horn, then jump back in.
Orchestra continues with no break.

CUT ON CUE (Lord): "Pay for this madness?"
— ORCH. STOP ABRUPTLY and ALMOST SEGUE to next [27B]...

Final Curtain

Bow Music

Exit Music

www.ingramcontent.com/pod-product-compliance
Lightning Source LLC
Chambersburg PA
CBHW080734300426
44114CB00019B/2591